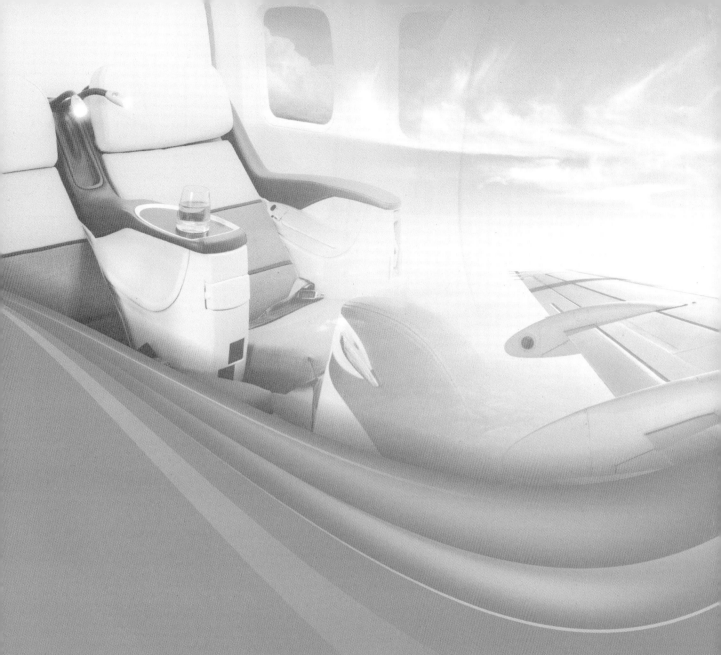

Practical English
for Airline Service

Preface

Practical English for Airline Service was written to help students improve their English and to pursue a cabin crew career. English proficiency is essential for people thinking of becoming part of a cabin crew. This book is especially aimed to develop the communicative abilities of the students. The dialogues have been carefully chosen to perform the various duties they will be taking over while working as a cabin crew member.

Practical English for Airline Service is designed for the sequence of a flight based on NCS (National Competency Standards). This book covers basic and essential English expressions from passenger boarding to passenger deplaning on the whole. Therefore, students will develop their English skills as well as understanding of airline service.

Each chapter consists of five parts:

Words - Key vocabulary words are listed with the English definition. These words are used and recycled in the chapter.

Useful Phrases – This section provides essential phrases students may use in real life situations. It will help to transform the original structure into various expressions.

Conversation - This section gives various dialogues using the phrases found in the words and useful phrases sections. It is followed by pair work, so that students can get the opportunity to put all they have learned into practice.

Build-up – It consists of a few exercises to review the key terms. It will provide extra practice for students to understand what they have learned.

Reading Comprehension - It gives reading materials related to the subject from each chapter. This section facilitates reading comprehension skills and also provides essential information about airlines. It is followed by a series of reading comprehension questions.

Answer Keys will be provided in the back of the book.

Construction

PRACTICAL ENGLISH FOR AIRLINE CABIN SERVICE

이 책은 항공서비스 관련 학과 학생들과 항공사 취업을 목표로 하는 취업 준비생, 그리고 현직 객실승무원을 대상으로 고객들에게 보다 질 높은 서비스를 제공하는데 도움을 주기 위한 '항공서비스 실용영어 회화 교재'입니다. 이 책은 항공객실 서비스 부분의 NCS 학습모듈을 기반으로 하고 있습니다.

모두 5장으로 구성되어 있으며, 각 장은 승객 탑승에서부터 하기 때까지의 다양한 상황을 승객과 객실승무원의 대화문으로 구성하였습니다. 특히 본격적인 영어 학습 전에, 학습자의 이해를 돕기 위해 객실 승무원의 업무와 항공 서비스 절차에 대한 내용을 간략히 우리말로 설명하였습니다. 또한 대화에 어울리는 사진과 일러스트 등의 다양한 시각적인 자료를 통해 흥미있게 영어학습을 할 수 있도록 하였습니다. 각 장은 [Words — Useful Phrases — Conversation — Pair work — Build up — Reading Comprehension]으로 구성되었습니다.

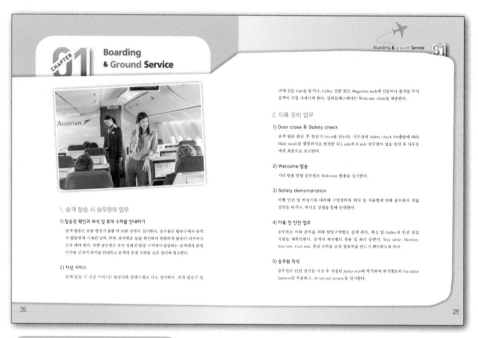

Introduction

각 장의 주제와 관련된 객실승무원의 업무와 기내서비스 절차 및 방법을 살펴볼 수 있는 부분으로, 객실승무원이 되기 위해 공부하는 분들이 전체적인 흐름을 파악하기 쉽게 하고자 개괄적인 설명을 우리말로 제공하였습니다.

Words

본격적인 학습에 들어가기 전 주제와 관련한 핵심 어휘들을 살펴봄으로써 학습을 준비합니다. 어휘의 의미를 영영풀이로 제시해서 영어식 사고를 하도록 돕고, 어휘를 활용할 수 있는 다양한 문장을 통해 의미를 재확인할 수 있습니다.

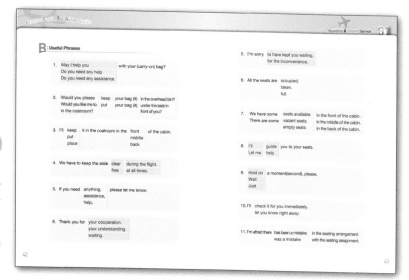

Useful Phrases

기내에서 자주 쓰이는 문형을 한눈에 보기 쉽게 정리하였습니다. 일정한 패턴의 문형에 어휘를 바꿔가면서 다양한 문장으로 활용해 볼 수 있습니다. 모든 문장이 자연스럽게 입에서 나올 수 있도록 반복적으로 학습해야 합니다.

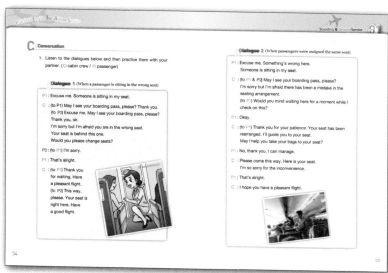

Conversation

각 장의 주제에 맞게 기내에서 실제 일어나는 다양한 상황을 승객과 객실 승무원의 대화를 통해 학습할 수 있습니다. 대화에 해당되는 mp3음성을 반복해서 들으며 표현을 익히기 바랍니다.

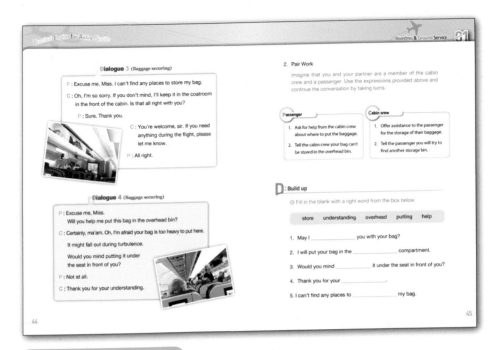

Pair Work

파트너와 승객과 객실승무원의 역할을 번갈아 해보면서 지시에 알맞게 대화를 연습해 보도록 합니다.
Conversation에서 학습한 어휘와 표현들을 다양하게 활용해 보는 것이 좋습니다.

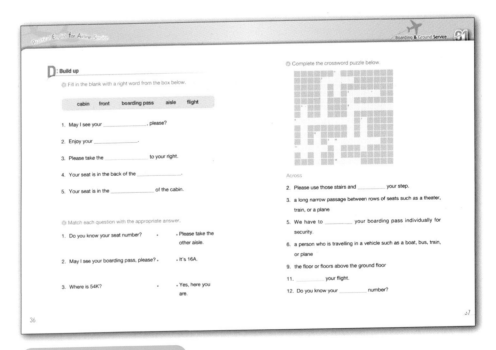

Build up

Conversation에서 공부한 내용들을 다시 복습해 볼 수 있습니다. 빈칸 추론, 대화 연습, 문장 완성하기, crossword puzzle 등의 다양한 문제 유형을 통해 학습한 내용을 재확인합니다.

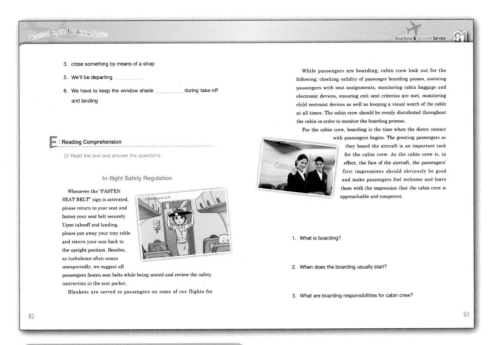

Reading Comprehension

각 장의 주제와 맞는 엄선된 영어 지문을 통해 영어 독해 실력을 향상시킬 뿐만 아니라 항공산업 전반에 관한 지식을 함양할 수 있습니다. 또한 관련된 문제를 풀면서 지문에 대한 이해를 재확인할 수 있도록 하였습니다.

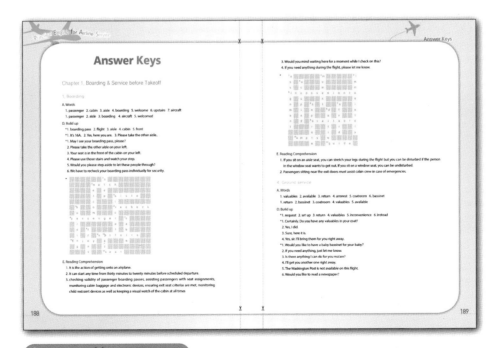

Answer Keys

각 장에서 학습한 내용에 대한 문제를 푼 후 질문에 적절하게 답변하였는지를 점검할 수 있도록 모범답안을 제공하였습니다.

Contents

PRACTICAL ENGLISH FOR AIRLINE CABIN SERVICE

NCS
(National Competency Standard)

1. 국가직무능력표준이란?

국가직무능력표준(NCS, National Competency Standard)은 산업현장에서 직무를 수행하기 위해 요구되는 지식, 기술, 태도 등의 내용을 국가가 체계화한 것이다.

2. 국가직무능력표준 개념도

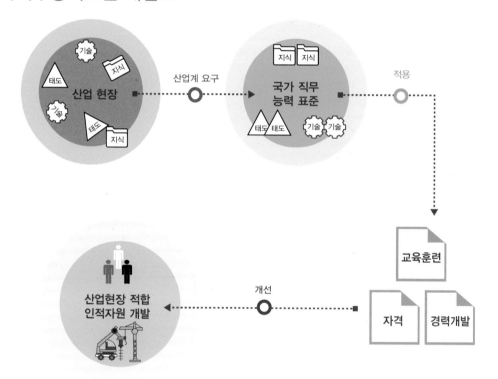

3. NCS 분류체계

대 분 류	중 분 류	소 분 류	세 분 류
12. 이용 · 숙박 · 여행 · 오락 · 스포츠	03. 관광 · 레저	01. 여행서비스	01. 여행상품개발
			02. 여행상품상담
			03. 국내여행안내
			04. 국외여행안내
			05. 항공객실서비스

4. 항공객실서비스 직무 개요

1) 직무 정의

항공객실서비스란 객실 안전관리, 승객 탑승 전 준비, 승객 탑승 서비스, 이륙 전 서비스, 비행 중 서비스, 착륙 전 서비스, 착륙 후 서비스, 승객 하기 후 관리, 응급환자 대처, 객실승무 관리를 하는 일이다.

2) 능력단위

순번	능 력 단 위
1	기내 안전관리
2	승객 탑승 전 준비
3	**승객 탑승 및 이륙 전 서비스**
4	**비행 중 서비스**
5	**착륙 전 서비스**
6	**착륙 후 서비스**
7	승객 하기 후 관리
8	**응급환자 대처**
9	객실승무 관리
10	기내음료 서비스
11	항공서비스 업무 기본
12	항공 기내방송 업무
13	고객만족 서비스
14	항공서비스 매너

3) 능력단위별 능력단위요소

분류번호	능력단위	수준	능력단위요소
1203010501_15v2	기내 안전관리	3	승객 탑승 전 안전 · 보안 점검하기
			항공기 이 · 착륙 전 안전 · 보안 관리하기
			비행 중 안전 · 보안 관리하기
			착륙 후 안전 · 보안 점검 · 관리
			비상사태 발생 시 대응하기
			상황별 안전안내 방송하기

분류번호	능력단위	수준	능력단위요소
1203010502_13v1	승객 탑승 전 준비	3	기내서비스용품 점검하기
			서비스 설비 및 기물 점검하기
			특별 서비스 요청사항 점검하기
1203010503_16v2	승객 탑승 및 이륙 전 서비스	3	탑승위치 대기하기
			탑승권 재확인하기
			좌석 안내하기
			수하물 정리 지원하기
			특수 고객 지원하기
1203010504_13v1	비행 중 서비스	3	기내음료 제공하기
			기내식 제공하기
			기내 오락물 제공하기
			면세품 판매하기
			객실 상태 점검하기
1203010505_16v2	착륙 전 서비스	3	입국 서류 배포 및 작성 지원하기
			기내 용품 회수하기
			기내 서비스 용품 및 면세품 재고 확인하기
1203010506_16v2	착륙 후 서비스	3	승객 하기 지원하기
			특수 고객 지원하기
1203010507_13v1	승객 하기 후 관리	3	유실물 점검하기
			잔류 승객 점검하기
			기내 설비 점검하기
			기내 용품 인수·인계하기
1203010508_13v1	응급환자 대처	3	응급환자 발생상황 파악·보고하기
			응급환자 초기 대응하기
			응급환자 후속 관리하기
			환자 대처 상황 기록하기
1203010509_16v2	객실승무 관리	4	객실 승무원별 근무 배정하기
			운항·객실간 정보 공유하기
			불만 승객 관리하기
			출·도착 서류 작성·관리하기
			객실서비스 관리하기

분류번호	능력단위	수준	능력단위요소
1203010510_16v1	기내음료 서비스	2	기내음료 파악하기
			기내음료 제공하기
1203010511_16v1	항공서비스 업무 기본	2	항공서비스 관련 서류 확인하기
			항공여객정보 확인하기
1203010512_16v1	항공 기내방송 업무	3	항공기내 방송 준비하기
			정상적 상황 방송하기
			비정상 상황 방송하기
			비상 상황 방송하기
1203010513_16v1	고객만족 서비스	3	서비스 마인드 함양하기
			이미지 메이킹하기
			불만고객 대처하기
1203010514_16v1	항공서비스 매너	2	기본 매너 갖추기
			항공서비스 매너 관리하기

4) 능력단위요소별 수행준거

(1) 승객 탑승 및 이륙전 서비스

분류번호 : 1203010503_16v2

능력단위 명칭 : **승객 탑승 및 이륙전 서비스**

능력단위 정의 : 승객 탑승 및 이륙전 서비스란 탑승위치 대기, 탑승권 재확인, 좌석 안내, 수하물
정리 지원, 특수 고객 지원, 탑승환영 안내 방송을 수행하는 능력이다.

능력단위요소	수 행 준 거
1203010503_16v2.1 탑승위치 대기하기	1.1. 객실 서비스 규정에 따라, 승객의 항공기 탑승 전, 각자에게 부여된 임무를 수행 하기 위하여 해당 근무지역에서 탑승을 위해 대기할 수 있다. 1.2 객실 서비스 규정에 따라 승객 탑승 시 대기 자세를 취할 수 있다. 1.3 객실 서비스 규정에 따라 승객 탑승 시 밝은 표정으로 환영 인사를 할 수 있다. 1.4 객실 서비스 규정에 따라 탑승 승객에 따른 눈높이 서비스 자세를 취할 수 있다. 【지 식】 ㅇ 객실 서비스 규정 이해 ㅇ 비행 전 업무절차 이해 ㅇ 승객 특성 이해

능력단위요소	수 행 준 거
	【기술】 ○ 객실 서비스 규정 활용 기술 ○ 승객 특성에 따른 인사, 표정 기술 ○ 승객 특성에 따른 대화 기술
	【태도】 ○ 밝은 태도 ○ 공손한 태도 ○ 명료한 태도
1203010503_16v2.2 탑승권 재확인하기	2.1 객실 서비스 규정에 따라, 승객의 출발 일시를 확인할 수 있다. 2.2 객실 서비스 규정에 따라, 승객의 목적지를 파악할 수 있다. 2.3 객실 서비스 규정에 따라, 승객의 좌석 등급을 구별할 수 있다. 2.4 객실 서비스 규정에 따라, 승객의 좌석번호를 확인할 수 있다.
	【지식】 ○ 객실 서비스 규정에 대한 이해 ○ 비행 전 업무절차에 대한 이해 ○ 객실 구조에 대한 이해 ○ 승객 특성에 대한 이해 ○ 항공 운송 관련 기본 지식(예약 · 발권, 운송, 운항, 정비, 기내식)
	【기술】 ○ 객실 서비스 근무규정 활용 기술 ○ 비행전 업무절차 규정 활용 기술 ○ 탑승권 판독 능력 ○ 승객과의 의사소통 기술 ○ 의전 관련 기술
	【태도】 ○ 공손한 태도 ○ 정확성 유지 ○ 신속한 태도
1203010503_16v2.3 좌석 안내하기	3.1 객실 서비스 규정에 따라, 승객들에게 지정된 좌석번호를 재확인할 수 있다. 3.2 객실 서비스 규정에 따라, 좌석 배열을 파악하고, 승객에게 정확한 좌석으로 안내할 수 있다. 3.3 객실 서비스 규정에 따라, 승객에게 좌석 설비 사용법을 안내할 수 있다. 3.4 객실 서비스 규정에 따라, 좌석 상태를 파악하여, 조치할 수 있다.
	【지식】 ○ 승무원 근무절차 이해 ○ 객실승무원의 근무규정 이해 ○ 비행 전 업무절차 이해 ○ 좌석 배열 이해 ○ 좌석의 특성 이해 ○ 좌석의 설비(이어폰잭, 독서등 등) 이해 ○ 좌석의 사용법

능력단위요소	수 행 준 거
	【기 술】 ○ 객실 서비스 규정활용 기술 ○ 좌석 벨트 착용 기술 ○ 오디오 비디오 작동 기술
	【태 도】 ○ 적극적인 태도 ○ 협조 노력 ○ 배려있는 태도
1203010503_16v2.4 수하물 정리 지원하기	4.1 객실 서비스 규정에 따라, 좌석 주변의 공간을 파악하여, 승객에게 객실 선반의 위치를 안내할 수 있다. 4.2 객실 서비스 규정에 따라, 안전하게 선반을 작동할 수 있다. 4.3 객실 서비스 규정에 따라, 수하물의 특성별로 보관하도록 안내할 수 있다. 4.4 객실 서비스 규정에 따라, 수하물을 안전하게 다룰 수 있다. 4.5 객실 서비스 규정에 따라, 수하물의 보관 위치를 기억하여, 승객에게 다시 전달할 수 있다.
	【지 식】 ○ 객실 서비스 규정 이해 ○ 좌석 하단 특성 이해 ○ 수하물 선반 사용 특성 이해 ○ 코트룸 특성 이해
	【기 술】 ○ 객실 서비스 근무규정 활용 기술 ○ 수하물 선반 사용 기술 ○ 코트룸 사용 기술 ○ 좌석 하단 사용 기술
	【태 도】 ○ 안전성 유지 노력 ○ 정중한 태도 ○ 유연한 태도 ○ 정확성 유지
1203010503_16v2.5 특수 고객 지원하기	5.1 객실 서비스 규정에 따라, 특수 고객 탑승 여부를 확인할 수 있다. 5.2 객실 서비스 규정에 따라, 특수 고객의 특성에 따른 인사를 하고, 좌석 안내할 수 있다. 5.3 객실 서비스 규정에 따라, 특수 고객에게 기내 설비 사용법을 안내할 수 있다. 5.4 객실 서비스 규정에 따라, 특수 고객에 대한 여행 편의를 제공할 수 있다.
	【지 식】 ○ 객실 서비스 규정 이해 ○ 비상 응급조치 이해 ○ 의전에 대한 지식 ○ 특수 승객의 특성 이해

Na Co St

능력단위요소	수 행 준 거
	【기 술】 ○ 객실 서비스 규정 활용 기술 ○ 탑승객과의 원활한 소통 기술 ○ 휠체어 사용 기술 ○ 특수 고객 응대 기술
	【태 도】 ○ 정중한 태도 ○ 사려 깊은 태도 ○ 인내성 있는 태도
1203010503_16v2.6 탑승 환영 안내방송하기	6.1 객실 서비스 규정에 따라 방송에 필요한 정보를 파악할 수 있다. 6.2 객실 서비스 규정에 따라 탑승환영 안내 방송에 필요한 언어를 구사할 수 있다. 6.3 객실 서비스 규정에 따라 탑승환영 안내 방송에 필요한 표준어 사용을 할 수 있어야 한다.
	【지 식】 ○ 객실 서비스 규정(안내) ○ 한국어, 영어 및 목적지 국가 언어(일본어, 중국어 등) 이해
	【기 술】 ○ 영어, 일어, 중국어 구사 능력 ○ 표준어 구사 기술 ○ 음성 표현 기술
	【태 도】 ○ 성실한 태도 ○ 정확성 유지 ○ 명료한 태도

(2) 비행 중 서비스

분류번호 : 1203010504_13v1

능력단위 명칭 : **비행 중 서비스**

능력단위 정의 : 비행 중 서비스란 기내음료제공, 기내식제공, 기내오락물제공, 면세품 판매, 객실
상태점검을 수행하는 능력이다.

능력단위요소	수 행 준 거
1203010504_13v1.1 기내음료 제공하기	1.1 객실 서비스 규정에 따라, 비알콜 음료(Cold Beverage, Hot Beverage)에 관한 정보를 승객에게 전달할 수 있다. 1.2 객실 서비스 규정에 따라, 다양한 칵테일 제조에 필요한 술의 종류와 첨가 음료에 관한 정보를 숙지하여, 제조할 수 있다. 1.3 객실 서비스 규정에 따라, 다양한 와인에 관한 정보를 파악하여, 서비스 및 회수할 수 있다.

능력단위요소	수 행 준 거
	【지 식】 o 칵테일 제조 및 서비스 이해 o 알콜 · 비알콜 음료에 대한 지식 o 테이블 매너 이해 o 와인에 대한 지식(원산지, 특성, 어울리는 음식, 서비스 방법) o 원산지별 커피종류와 로스팅 등 음용 방법 이해
	【기 술】 o 칵테일 제조 능력 o 와인 서비스 능력 o 음료서비스 기물 사용 기술(머들러, 캐리어, 칵테일 종류에 따른 글라스 선정, 칵테일 픽, 코스터 등)
	【태 도】 o 적극적 자세 유지 o 고객 특성에 대한 이해 노력
1203010504_13v1.2 기내식 제공하기	2.1 객실 서비스 규정에 따라, 기내에서 제공되는 식사를 위한 세팅(Setting) 및 데우기(Heating) 등을 수행할 수 있다. 2.2 특별서비스요청서(SSR: Special Service Request)에 따라 특별식을 확인 후, 서비스 및 회수할 수 있다. 2.3 객실 서비스 규정에 따라, 승객 선호를 확인하여, 테이블 매너에 따른 기내식을 서비스 및 회수할 수 있다. **【지 식】** o 테이블 매너 이해 o 고객 만족 서비스 이해 o 기내식 서비스를 위한 기물의 종류와 사용법 o 특별식 종류와 특성 이해 **【기 술】** o 세련된 서비스 매너 기술 o 코스별 서비스 기술 o 세팅(Setting) 기술 o 데우기(Heating) 기술 **【태 도】** o 세심한 태도 o 배려있는 태도 o 겸손한 태도 o 친절한 태도
1203010504_13v1.3 기내 오락물 제공하기	3.1 객실 서비스 규정에 따라, 기내에서 제공되는 오락물 상영을 위한 기내 시설물과 기물을 사용할 수 있다. 3.2 객실 서비스 규정에 따라, 비행 중 서비스되는 상영물에 관한 종류와 내용을 고객에게 전달할 수 있다. 3.3 객실 서비스 규정에 따라, 조명 및 객실상태를 점검하고, 오락물을 제공할 수 있다.

능력단위요소	수 행 준 거
	【지 식】 ○ 객실 오락설비(오디오, 비디오 등) 이해 ○ 객실 오락물에 관한 지식
	【기 술】 ○ 오락설비 사용 기술 ○ 조명기기 조절 기술
	【태 도】 ○ 배려있는 태도 ○ 적극적 자세 유지 ○ 친절한 태도
1203010504_13v1.4 면세품 판매하기	4.1 객실 서비스 규정에 따라, 면세품 판매를 위한 기본적인 상품을 세팅하고, 판매할 수 있다. 4.2 객실 서비스 규정에 따라, 국가별 면세품 구매 한도에 관한 정보를 전달할 수 있다. 4.3 객실 서비스 규정에 따라, 면세품 판매 전·후 재고파악 및 인수인계를 위한 서류를 정리할 수 있다.
	【지 식】 ○ 국가별 면세 한도액 규정 이해 ○ 기내 면세품에 관한 정보 이해 ○ 객실 서비스 규정 이해
	【기 술】 ○ 효율적인 판매를 위한 세팅 기술 ○ 신용카드 리더기 사용 기술 ○ 인수인계를 위한 행정 서류 정리 기술
	【태 도】 ○ 세심한 태도 ○ 정확성 유지 ○ 친절한 태도
1203010504_13v1.5 객실 상태 점검하기	5.1 객실 서비스 규정에 따라, 고객 서비스를 위해 객실 시설물을 수시로 점검하고, 조치를 할 수 있다. 5.2 객실 서비스 규정에 따라 기내식 서비스 후 객실 통로 및 주변을 청결히 할 수 있다. 5.3 객실 서비스 규정에 따라 승객의 쾌적한 여행을 위해 객실 내 온도 및 조명을 관리할 수 있다.
	【지 식】 ○ 화장실 용품사용법 ○ 화장실 설비에 관한 지식 ○ 조리실(Galley) 내 기물 사용법 ○ 조리실(Galley) 내 용품에 관한 지식

능력단위요소	수 행 준 거
	【기술】 ○ 조리실(Galley) 내 용품 정돈 기술 ○ 인수인계 용품의 확인과 정리 기술 ○ 객실 온도 및 조명 조절 기술
	【태도】 ○ 성실한 태도 ○ 청결함 유지

(3) 착륙 전 서비스

분류번호 : 1203010505_16v2

능력단위 명칭 : **착륙 전 서비스**

능력단위 정의 : 착륙 전 서비스란 입국서류 배포 및 작성 지원, 기내서비스용품 회수, 기내 서비스용품 및 면세품 재고 확인, 목적지 도착 안내방송을 수행하는 능력이다.

능력단위요소	수 행 준 거
1203010505_16v2.1 입국 서류 배포 및 작성 지원하기	1.1 객실 서비스 규정에 의해, 담당구역별 도착지 입국에 필요한 서류를 배포할 수 있다. 1.2 객실 서비스 규정에 따라, 도착지 국가의 출입국 규정을 숙지하여 승객에게 정확히 안내할 수 있다. 1.3 객실 서비스 규정에 따라 도착 전 입국에 필요한 서류의 작성 여부를 점검하고, 조치할 수 있다. 1.4 객실 서비스 규정에 의해 특수 고객에게 필요한 서류 작성에 협조할 수 있다. **【지식】** ○ 객실 서비스 규정 이해 ○ 국가별 출입국 규정에 대한 지식 ○ 국가별 입국 서류 작성법에 대한 지식 ○ 고객 특성 **【기술】** ○ 국가별 출입국 서류 작성기술 ○ 외국어 능력 ○ 문서작성 기술 **【태도】** ○ 고객지향적인 태도 ○ 관련 규정사항 준수 ○ 적극적인 태도 ○ 친절한 자세 ○ 정확성 유지

능력단위요소	수 행 준 거
1203010505_16v2.2 기내 용품 회수하기	2.1 객실 서비스 규정에 의해, 서비스한 기내 용품과 회수된 기내 용품의 수량을 파악할 수 있다. 2.2 객실 서비스 규정에 의해, 회수된 기내 용품의 상태를 확인하여, 상태별로 분리할 수 있다. 2.3 객실 서비스 규정에 의해, 기내 용품 소지 승객에 대해 회수 안내할 수 있다. 【지 식】 ○ 객실 서비스 규정 ○ 기내 용품에 대한 지식 【기 술】 ○ 의사소통기술 ○ 기내용품 관리 기술 【태 도】 ○ 정확성 유지 ○ 친절한 태도 ○ 적극적인 태도
1203010505_16v2.3 기내 서비스 용품 및 면세품 재고 확인하기	3.1 객실 서비스 규정에 따라, 기내 판매 업무를 종료하고, 면세품 재고를 확인할 수 있다. 3.2 객실 서비스 규정에 따라, 면세품에 대한 상태를 확인하여, 필요 조치를 취할 수 있다. 3.3 객실 서비스 규정에 따라 서비스 종료 후, 서비스 용품 재고를 확인할 수 있다. 3.4 객실 서비스 규정에 따라 하기 시 필요한 조치 사항과 교대팀에게 필요한 전달 상항을 기록할 수 있다. 【지 식】 ○ 객실 서비스 규정 이해 ○ 면세품에 대한 지식 ○ DB자료(서비스용품별) 이해 【기 술】 ○ 기내서비스용품 목록 작성기술 ○ 서류 작성 기술 【태 도】 ○ 공정한 태도 ○ 정확성 유지 ○ 관련 규정사항 준수 ○ 배려있는 태도 ○ 적극적인 태도
1203010505_16v2.4 목적지 도착 안내방송하기	4.1 객실 서비스 규정에 따라 방송에 필요한 정보를 파악할 수 있다. 4.2 객실 서비스 규정에 따라 목적지 도착 안내방송에 필요한 언어를 구사할 수 있다. 4.3 객실 서비스 규정에 따라 목적지 도착 안내방송에 필요한 표준어 사용을 할 수 있다.

능력단위요소	수 행 준 거
	【지 식】 ○ 객실 서비스 규정(안내) 이해 ○ 한국어, 영어 및 목적지 국가 언어(일본어, 중국어 등) 이해
	【기 술】 ○ 영어, 일어, 중국어 구사 능력 ○ 표준어 구사 기술 ○ 음성 표현 기술
	【태 도】 ○ 성실한 태도 ○ 정확성 유지 ○ 명료한 태도

(4) 착륙 후 서비스

분류번호 : 1203010506_16v2

능력단위 명칭 : **착륙 후 서비스**

능력단위 정의 : 착륙 후 서비스란 착륙 후부터 승객하기 전까지 도착 안내방송, 승객 하기 지원, 특수 고객지원을 수행하는 능력이다.

능력단위요소	수 행 준 거
	1.1 객실 서비스 규정에 따라 착륙 후 도착 안내방송(Farewell) 실시할 수 있다. 1.2 객실 서비스 규정에 따라, 여권과 입국서류 소지 안내 방송을 실시할 수 있다. 1.3 객실 서비스 규정에 의거, 해당 공항에 따른 상황별 안내방송을 할 수 있다.
	【지 식】 ○ 객실 서비스 규정 이해 ○ 도착지 공항별 상황 이해 ○ 도착지공항 입출국 이해
1203010506_16v2.1 도착 안내방송하기	**【기 술】** ○ 외국어능력 ○ 정보검색능력 ○ 기내방송시스템 사용기술 ○ 방송문에 대한 방송 능력
	【태 도】 ○ 명료한 태도 ○ 고객 지향적 사고 노력 ○ 관련 규정사항 준수

능력단위요소	수 행 준 거
	2.1 도착지 공항 규정에 따라 검역 또는 세관의 허가가 필요한지 확인할 수 있다. 2.2 객실 서비스 규정에 따라 승객 하기 시, 감사하는 마음으로 하기 인사를 실시 할 수 있다. 2.3 객실 서비스 규정에 의해 승객의 짐 운반 등을 적극적으로 도움을 줄 수 있다.
1203010506_16v2.2 승객 하기 지원하기	【지 식】 ○ 객실 서비스 규정 이해 ○ 도착지 입출국 정보 이해 ○ 도착지 공항시설 이해
	【기 술】 ○ 의사소통 기술 ○ 외국어 능력 ○ 인사 기술
	【태 도】 ○ 공손한 태도 ○ 적극적 자세 유지 ○ 신속한 태도
	3.1 객실 서비스 규정에 따라 지상직원에게 여객 및 화물 운송 관련 서류(Ship pouch)를 인계하고, 중요 승객이나 특별 승객에 대한 정보를 구두로 먼저 알려 줄 수 있다. 3.2 객실 서비스 규정에 따라 응급환자, VIP, F/C, C/C, Y/C, UM(비동반소아), Stretcher(환자) 승객 순으로 신속히 하기가 이루어질 수 있도록 안내할 수 있다. 3.3 객실 서비스 규정에 따라 특수 고객을 위해, 적극적으로 게이트(Gate)까지 지원 할 수 있다.
1203010506_16v2.3 특수 고객 지원하기	【지 식】 ○ 도착지 공항 입출국에 대한 지식 ○ 특수고객별 특성 이해 ○ 휠체어 사용 방법
	【기 술】 ○ 휠체어 사용기술 ○ 외국어 및 커뮤니케이션 능력 ○ 고객 DB활용 기술 ○ 특수 고객에 대한 이동수행 능력
	【태 도】 ○ 공손한 태도 ○ 정확하고 신속한 태도 ○ 배려있는 태도 ○ 조심성 유지

(5) 응급환자 대처

분류번호 : 1203010508_13v1

능력단위 명칭 : **응급환자 대처**

능력단위 정의 : 응급환자 대처란 응급환자 발생상황 파악·보고, 응급환자 초기 대응, 응급환자 후
속관리, 환자 대처상황 기록을 수행하는 능력이다.

능 력 단 위 요 소	수 행 준 거
1203010508_13v1.1 응급환자 발생상황 파악·보고하기	1.1 객실 서비스 및 객실 안전 규정에 따라 기내 환자 발생 여부를 파악할 수 있다. 1.2 객실 서비스 및 객실 안전 규정에 따라 환자에 대한 정보를 신속하게 상급자에게 보고할 수 있다. 1.3 객실 서비스 및 객실 안전 규정에 따라 환자에 대한 정보를 공유하도록 할 수 있다.
	【지 식】 ○ 환자 증세에 대한 지식
	【기 술】 ○ 상황 보고 능력
	【태 도】 ○ 정확한 태도 ○ 꼼꼼함 유지 ○ 세밀한 태도 ○ 신속한 태도
1203010508_13v1.2 응급환자 초기 대응하기	2.1 객실 서비스 및 객실 안전 규정에 따라 응급 처치할 수 있다. 2.2 객실 서비스 및 객실 안전 규정에 따라 환자의 응급 상태를 확인하고, 탑승 의사와 의료진을 신속하게 찾을 수 있다. 2.3 객실 서비스 및 객실 안전 규정에 따라 응급치료 장비를 탑승 의사의 협조를 구해 활용할 수 있도록 조치할 수 있다.
	【지 식】 ○ 응급환자 대응매뉴얼 이해 ○ 응급처치 이해 ○ 의료 장비 기본 지식
	【기 술】 ○ 응급처치 능력 ○ 고객 심리분석 능력
	【태 도】 ○ 신속한 태도 ○ 정확한 태도

능력단위요소	수 행 준 거
	3.1 응급환자 대응매뉴얼에 따라 응급환자 상태가 악화되지 않도록 관리할 수 있다. 3.2 응급환자 발생에 따라 일반 탑승자의 쾌적한 여행이 방해되지 않도록 조치할 수 있다. 3.3 착륙 후 응급환자 대응매뉴얼에 따라 공항과의 협조체제가 순조롭게 진행될 수 있게 조치 할 수 있다.
1203010508_13v1.3 응급환자 후속 관리하기	【지 식】 ㅇ 응급환자 응대에 대한 지식
	【기 술】 ㅇ 응급 환자 응대 능력 ㅇ 응급 환자 관리 능력
	【태 도】 ㅇ 세심한 태도 ㅇ 편안한 태도
	4.1 객실 서비스 및 객실 안전 규정에 따라 응급환자 발생 시 조치 내용과 상태를 기록할 수 있다. 4.2 객실 서비스 및 객실 안전 규정에 따라 응급환자 관련 후속 조치내용을 기록할 수 있다. 4.3 객실 서비스 및 객실 안전 규정에 따라 응급환자의 공항 인계인수 내용을 기록할 수 있다. 4.4 객실 서비스 및 객실 안전 규정에 따라 비행 종료 후 환자 조치 내역을 기록하여 회사에 보고하고 향후 환자관리에 참고가 되도록 할 수 있다.
1203010508_13v1.4 환자 대처 상황 기록하기	【지 식】 ㅇ 응급환자 기본조치에 대한 지식 ㅇ 메디칼 레코드 이해
	【기 술】 ㅇ 단계별 구별 기술 ㅇ 조치 요약 기술
	【태 도】 ㅇ 꼼꼼함 유지 ㅇ 정확한 태도

Boarding
& Ground
Service

Boarding
& Ground Service

1. 승객 탑승 시 승무원의 업무

1) 탑승권 확인과 좌석 및 휴대 수하물 안내하기

승객 탑승은 보통 항공기 출발 약 30분 전부터 실시한다. 승무원은 탑승구에서 승객의 탑승권에 기재된 날짜, 편명, 좌석번호 등을 확인하여 원활하게 탑승이 이루어지도록 해야 한다. 또한 승무원은 각자 정해진 담당 구역에서 탑승하는 승객에게 환영인사를 건네며 좌석을 안내하고 승객의 휴대 수하물 보관 정리에 협조한다.

2) 지상 서비스

승객 탑승 시 지상 서비스는 항공사와 클래스별로 다소 상이하다. 대개 탑승구 입

구에 신문 Cart를 놓거나, Galley 선반 또는 Magazine rack에 신문이나 잡지를 두어 승객이 직접 가져가게 한다. 상위클래스에서는 Welcome drink를 제공한다.

2. 이륙 준비 업무

1) Door close 후 Safety check

승객 탑승 완료 후 항공기 Door를 닫는다. 사무장의 Safety check PA방송에 따라 Slide mode를 팽창위치로 변경한 뒤 L side와 R side 승무원이 상호 점검 후 사무장에게 최종으로 보고한다.

2) Welcome 방송

기내 방송 담당 승무원은 Welcome 방송을 실시한다.

3) Safety demonstration

비행 안전 및 비상시를 대비해 구명장비의 위치 및 사용법에 대해 승무원이 직접 실연을 하거나, 비디오 상영을 통해 안내한다.

4) 이륙 전 안전 업무

승무원은 이륙 준비를 위해 담당구역별로 승객 좌석, 객실 및 Galley의 안전 점검 사항을 재확인한다. 승객의 좌석벨트 착용 및 좌석 등받이, Tray table, Monitor, Arm rest, Foot rest, 휴대 수하물 등의 정위치를 반드시 확인하도록 한다.

5) 승무원 착석

승무원은 안전 점검을 마친 후 지정된 Jump seat에 착석하여 좌석벨트와 Shoulder harness를 착용하고, 30 second review를 실시한다.

Boarding

A : Words

✿ Match the words to the meanings.

| boarding | upstairs | passenger | welcome |
| aircraft | cabin | aisle | |

1. _____ : a person who is travelling in a vehicle such as a boat, bus, train, or plane

2. _____ : a private room in a ship, boat, or plane

3. _____ : a long narrow passage between rows of seats such as a theater, train, or a plane

4. _____ : the act of getting on a train, ship, or aircraft to travel somewhere

5. _____ : to greet someone in a friendly or polite way

6. _____ : the floor or floors above the ground floor

7. _____ : a vehicle that is able to fly

B : Useful Phrases

1. It's | good | to have you on board.
       | nice |

2. May I | see your boarding pass? |
         | help you? |

3. Please | take | this | aisle.
          | go down | that |
          | proceed to | the other |

4. Your seat is in the | front | of the cabin | on the left.
                       | middle | | on the right.
                       | back |

5. It's | an aisle | seat.
        | a window |

6. Have a | good | flight.
          | nice |
          | wonderful |

C : Conversation

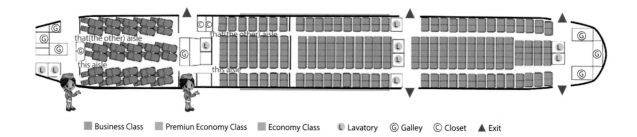

Business Class ■ Premiun Economy Class ■ Economy Class Ⓛ Lavatory Ⓖ Galley Ⓒ Closet ▲ Exit

1. Listen to the dialogues below and then practice them with your partner. (C: cabin crew / P: passenger)

Dialogue 1 (Boarding pass check)

C : Good afternoon. Welcome aboard.
    May I see your boarding pass, please?

P : Here it is.

C : Your seat number is 56A. Please take the aisle to your left.

P : Thank you.

C : You're welcome. Have a good flight.

Dialogue 2 (Boarding pass check)

C : Good morning, sir. It's good to have you on board.
Would you show me your boarding pass, please?

P : I know where my seat is. It's 48C.

C : I am sorry but we have to check your boarding pass
individually for security.

P : All right. Here it is.

C : Thank you for your cooperation.
Your seat is in the middle of the
cabin on your right.

Dialogue 3 (Seating guide)

C : Good morning. It's nice to have you on board.
What is your seat number?

P : It's 31C.

C : It's over there. Your seat is in front of
the cabin on your left side.
It's an aisle seat.

P : Thanks.

C : You're welcome. Have a nice flight.

Dialogue 4 (Seating guide)

C : Good evening, sir. Welcome to K Air.

P : Good evening. Where is 54K?

C : Please proceed to the other aisle. Your seat is in the back of the cabin on your right. It's a window seat.

P : Thanks a lot.

C : My pleasure. Enjoy your flight.

Dialogue 5 (Seating guide)

C : Good afternoon. Welcome aboard.
   Let me see your boarding pass, please.

P : Yes, here you are.

C : It's 16A. Your seat is upstairs.
   Please use those stairs and watch your step.

P : Thank you.

C : You're welcome. Have a good flight.

Dialogue 6 (Seating guide)

C : Excuse me, ma'am. Would you please
step aside to let these people through?

P : Oh, I'm sorry.

C : That's alright. Thank you.

2. Pair Work

Imagine that you and your partner are a member of the cabin crew and a passenger. Use the expressions provided above and continue the conversation by taking turns.

Cabin crew

Greet the passenger.
Ask the passenger to show his or her boarding pass.
Guide the passenger to his or her seat.

Passenger

Greet the cabin crew.
Show the boarding pass to the cabin crew.
Ask the cabin crew for help with finding your seat.

D : Build up

✿ Fill in the blank with a right word from the box below.

| cabin | front | boarding pass | aisle | flight |

1. May I see your _____, please?

2. Enjoy your _____.

3. Please take this _____ to your right.

4. Your seat is in the back of the _____.

5. Your seat is in the _____ of the cabin.

✿ Match each question with the appropriate answer.

1. Do you know your seat number? •   • Please take the other aisle.

2. May I see your boarding pass, please? •   • It's 16A.

3. Where is 54K? •   • Yes, here you are.

❈ Unscramble the words to make sentences.

1. pass,　May　see　please?　boarding　your　I

   ⇨ _____

2. the　on　Please　left.　take　other　your　aisle

   ⇨ _____

3. in the front　Your seat　on your left.　is　of the cabin

   ⇨ _____

4. use　Please　watch　those　and　step.　your　stairs

   ⇨ _____

5. these people through?　Would you please　to let　step aside

   ⇨ _____

6. individually　have to recheck　for security.　We　your boarding pass

   ⇨ _____

Complete the crossword puzzle below.

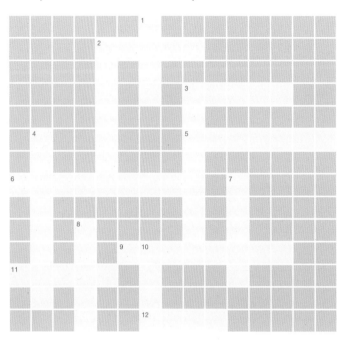

Across

2. Please use those stairs and _____ your step.

3. a long narrow passage between rows of seats such as a theater, train, or a plane

5. We have to _____ your boarding pass individually for security.

6. a person who is travelling in a vehicle such as a boat, bus, train, or plane

9. the floor or floors above the ground floor

11. _____ your flight.

12. Do you know your _____ number?

Down

1. Would you please _____ aside to let these people through?

2. to greet someone in a friendly or polite way

3. a vehicle that is able to fly

4. the act of getting on a train, ship, or aircraft to travel somewhere

7. a private room in a ship, boat, or plane

8. Your seat is in the _____ of the cabin.

10. May I see your boarding _____, please?

E : Reading Comprehension

✿ Read the text and answer the questions.

Boarding

Boarding is the action of getting onto an airplane. It can start any time from thirty minutes to twenty minutes before scheduled departure depending on the type of the plane, number of passengers, and whether it is a domestic or an international flight. Several airlines use priority boarding for passengers traveling with small children, first and business class passengers, frequent flyers, and certain card holders.

While passengers are boarding, cabin crew look out for the following: checking validity of passenger boarding passes, assisting passengers with seat assignments, monitoring cabin baggage and electronic devices, ensuring exit seat criterias are met, monitoring child restraint devices as well as keeping a visual watch of the cabin at all times. The cabin crew should be evenly distributed throughout the cabin in order to monitor the boarding process.

For the cabin crew, boarding is the time when the direct contact with passengers begins. The greeting passengers as they board the aircraft is an important task for the cabin crew. As the cabin crew is, in effect, the face of the aircraft, the passengers' first impressions should obviously be good and make passengers feel welcome and leave them with the impression that the cabin crew is approachable and competent.

1. What is boarding?

2. When does the boarding usually start?

3. What are boarding responsibilities for cabin crew?

 **Baggage securing**

A : Words

⚙ Match the words to the meanings.

| seat | overhead bin | compartment | coatroom | baggage |

1. _____ : a container above the seats used to store baggage

2. _____ : something made to sit on such as a chair

3. _____ : a room in which coats and other articles may be left temporarily

4. _____ : separate spaces used for keeping things in

5. _____ : trunks or suitcases to carry belongings for traveling

⚙ Complete the sentences with the correct word or words.

1. Please return to your _____ and fasten your seatbelt.

2. Would you like me to keep your coat in the _____?

3. Please place your bags into the overhead _____.

4. Where is the _____ claim area?

B: Useful Phrases

1. May I help you   with your (carry-on) bag?
   Do you need any help
   Do you need any assistance

2. Would you please   keep   your bag (it)   in the overhead bin?
   Would you like me to   put   your bag (it)   under the seat in
                                                   front of you?
                                                   in the coatroom?

3. I'll   keep   it in the coatroom in the   front   of the cabin.
          put   middle
          place   back

4. We have to keep the aisle   clear   during the flight.
                                free   at all times.

5. If you need   anything,   please let me know.
                 assistance,
                 help,

6. Thank you for   your cooperation.
                   your understanding.
                   waiting.

C : Conversation

1. Listen to the dialogues below and then practice them with your partner. (C: cabin crew / P: passenger)

Dialogue 1 (Baggage securing)

C : Good afternoon. May I help you with your bag, ma'am?

P : Please, thank you.

C : I will keep it in the overhead compartment.

P : Thanks a lot.

C : You're welcome, ma'am.

Dialogue 2 (Baggage securing)

C : Excuse me. Are these all your bags?

P : Yes, they are. Is there any problem?

C : I'm sorry but we have to keep the aisle clear at all times.

    Would you please put them in the overhead bin?

P : Oh, I see.

C : I'll help you. Thank you for your cooperation.

Dialogue 3 (Baggage securing)

P : Excuse me, Miss. I can't find any places to store my bag.

C : Oh, I'm so sorry. If you don't mind, I'll keep it in the coatroom in the front of the cabin. Is that all right with you?

P : Sure. Thank you.

C : You're welcome, sir. If you need anything during the flight, please let me know.

P : All right.

Dialogue 4 (Baggage securing)

P : Excuse me, Miss.

Will you help me put this bag in the overhead bin?

C : Certainly, ma'am. Oh, I'm afraid your bag is too heavy to put here.

It might fall out during turbulence.

Would you mind putting it under the seat in front of you?

P : Not at all.

C : Thank you for your understanding.

2. Pair Work

Imagine that you and your partner are a member of the cabin crew and a passenger. Use the expressions provided above and continue the conversation by taking turns.

Passenger

1. Ask for help from the cabin crew about where to put the baggage.

2. Tell the cabin crew your bag can't be stored in the overhead bin.

Cabin crew

1. Offer assistance to the passenger for the storage of their baggage.

2. Tell the passenger you will try to find another storage bin.

D: Build up

Fill in the blank with a right word from the box below.

| store | understanding | overhead | putting | help |

1. May I _____ you with your bag?

2. I will put your bag in the _____ compartment.

3. Would you mind _____ it under the seat in front of you?

4. Thank you for your _____.

5. I can't find any places to _____ my bag.

❀ Unscramble the words to make sentences.

1. during the flight.   have to keep   We   the aisle clear

   ⇨ _____

2. please   If you   during the flight,   let me know.   need anything

   ⇨ _____

3. of the cabin.   in the coatroom   in the front   I'll keep it

   ⇨ _____

4. you   please   Would   put   the   them   in   overhead bin?

   ⇨ _____

❀ Complete the crossword puzzle below.

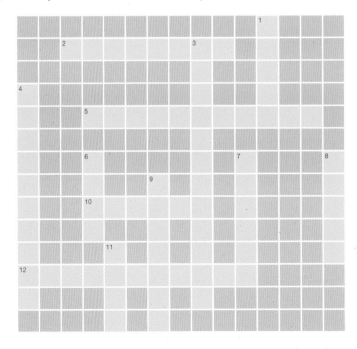

Across

2. a room in which coats and other articles may be left temporarily

5. separate spaces used for keeping things in

10. I'm _____ your bag is too heavy to put here.

12. Thank you for your _____.

Down

1. I can't find any places to _____ my bag.

3. a container above the seats used to store baggage

4. Do you need any _____ with your bag?

6. something made to sit on such as a chair

7. Please _____ your seatbelt.

8. We have to keep the aisle _____ at all times.

9. trunks or suitcases to carry belongings for traveling

11. Will you _____ me put this bag in the overhead bin?

E : Reading Comprehension

✿ Read the text and answer the questions.

Allowed to bring

Free baggage allowances

Free baggage allowances regarding size, weight, and quantity of baggage vary with passenger itineraries, seating seats, and SKYPASS membership grades.

The maximum size (width + height + depth) is 158cm/62in and the maximum weight per bag is 23kg/ 50lb or 32kg/70lb depending on your ticket class and itineraries. Bags between 23 and 32kg (51–70lb) may incur additional charges depending on your allowance.

Additional carry-on allowances

One additional personal carry-on item - laptop, briefcase, handbag - is permitted for Economy Class. (Total weight of carry-on bag and additional allowance should not exceed 12kg.)

Seating Class	Pieces	Total Weight
First/Prestige		18kg/40lb
Economy		12kg/25lb

Dimensions Limits

- 55(A)×20(B)×40(C) cm
- or a total sum of less than 115cm per piece

Carrying on musical instruments.

If the size of your musical instrument is less than 115cm (45in.) - such as a violin - you may carry it on free of charge. Larger instruments are permitted as carry-on items but an additional seat will need to be purchased to accommodate each item.

Carry-on baggage storage

All carry-ons must be able to be stored completely in an overhead bin or under the seat in front of you. Please double-check to make sure you have all of your personal items before leaving the aircraft.

www.koreanair.com

1. How many carry-on items can each passenger bring on board?

2. What is the maximum size and the maximum weight per bag, for the free baggage allowances?

3. Where should carry-on items be stored?

3 Seating arrangement

A : Words

✿ Match the words to the meanings.

arrange separate empty inconvenience assignment occupy

1. _____ : being apart

2. _____ : an act of distributing something to designated places

3. _____ : place something in proper or required order

4. _____ : someone is using something such as a room or seat, so that it is not available for anyone else.

5. _____ : something that causes problems or difficulties

6. _____ : vacant, containing nothing

✿ Complete the sentences with the correct word or words.

1. Should I buy a _____ seat for my child?

2. We're very sorry for any _____ it has caused you.

3. Can you _____ a seat for this flight?

4. Any person 2 years or older should _____ a seat when travelling on Korean Air.

5. You may change your seat _____ through the Internet.

B : Useful Phrases

1. I am | afraid | you | are | in the wrong seat.
     | sorry | | might be |

2. Your seat is right | behind | this one.
                      | in front of |
                      | over there. |

3. Would you | please change | seats?
             | mind changing |

4. Would you | please wait | here for a moment while I check on this?
             | mind waiting |

5. I'm sorry | to have kept you waiting.
              | for the inconvenience.

6. All the seats are | occupied.
                     | taken.
                     | full.

7. We have some | seats available | in the front of the cabin.
   There are some | vacant seats | in the middle of the cabin.
                   | empty seats | in the back of the cabin.

8. I'll | guide | you to your seats.
   Let me | help |

9. Hold on | a moment(second), please.
   Wait
   Just

10. I'll | check it for you | immediately.
         | let you know | right away.

11. I'm afraid there | has been a mistake | in the seating arrangement.
                     | was a mistake | with the seating assignment.

C : Conversation

1. Listen to the dialogues below and then practice them with your partner. (C: cabin crew / P: passenger)

Dialogue 1 (When a passenger is sitting in the wrong seat)

P1 : Excuse me. Someone is sitting in my seat.

C : (to P1) May I see your boarding pass, please? Thank you.
(to P2) Excuse me. May I see your boarding pass, please?
Thank you, sir.
I'm sorry but I'm afraid you are in the wrong seat.
Your seat is behind this one.
Would you please change seats?

P2 : (to P1) I'm sorry.

P1 : That's alright.

C : (to P1) Thank you
for waiting. Have
a pleasant flight.
(to P2) This way,
please. Your seat is
right here. Have
a good flight.

© www.hanol.co.kr

Dialogue 2 (When passengers were assigned the same seat)

P1 : Excuse me. Something's wrong here.
Someone is sitting in my seat.

C : (to P1 & P2) May I see your boarding pass, please?
I'm sorry but I'm afraid there has been a mistake in the
seating arrangement.
(to P1) Would you mind waiting here for a moment while I
check on this?

P1 : Okay.

C : (to P1) Thank you for your patience. Your seat has been
rearranged. I'll guide you to your seat.
May I help you take your bags to your seat?

P1 : No, thank you. I can manage.

C : Please come this way. Here is your seat.
I'm so sorry for the inconvenience.

P1 : That's alright.

C : I hope you have a pleasant flight.

Dialogue 3 (When passengers want to sit together)

P : Excuse me, my friend and I are seating in separate seats.
Do you think it's possible for us to sit together?

C : I'm sorry to hear that. I'll check if there are any vacant seats after boarding is finished. Wait a moment, please.

P : Okay.

C : Thank you for waiting. We have some seats available in the back of the cabin.
Would that be alright with you?

P : Sure.

C : I'll help you to your seats. This way, please.

Dialogue 4 (When passengers want to sit together)

P1 : Excuse me. My mother is sitting over there.
Is there any way we can sit together?

C : Wait a moment, please. I'll check it for you.
I am very sorry but all the seats are occupied.
Where is your mother sitting now?

P1 : Over there. 40C.

C : I'll go and ask the passenger sitting next to your mother.
Just a moment, please.

(to P2) Excuse me, sir. I'm very sorry to bother you.

The lady over there wants to sit together with her mother.

Would you mind changing seats so they can sit together?

P2 : No, I don't. Where should I sit?

C : Thank you so much, sir. This way, please.

(to P1) Ma'am, this gentleman is willing to change seats with you.

P1 : (to P2) Thank you very much.

P2 : No problem.

C : (to P2) I'm very sorry for the inconvenience, sir.

If you need anything during the flight, please let me know.

P2 : Okay. Thank you.

2. Pair Work

Imagine that you and your partner are a member of the cabin crew and a passenger. Use the expressions provided above and continue the conversation by taking turns.

Passenger

1. Tell the cabin crew someone is sitting in your seat.

2. Tell the cabin crew you and your companion have separate seats.

Cabin crew

1. Check boarding passes of the two passengers and solve the situation.

2. Offer assistance by rearranging seats.

D : Build up

✤ Fill in the blank with a right word from the box below.

| inconvenience | separate | behind | rearranged |

1. My friend and I are seating in _____ seats.

2. Your seat is _____ this one.

3. Your seat has been _____.

4. I'm so sorry for the _____.

✤ Unscramble the words to make sentences.

1. of the cabin.   We have   in the back   available   some seats

   ⇨ _____

2. seating arrangement.   I'm afraid   a mistake   in the   there has been

   ⇨ _____

3. waiting here   check on this?   while I   for a moment   Would you mind

   ⇨ _____

4. please   If you   during the flight,   let me know.   need anything

   ⇨ _____

Complete the crossword puzzle below.

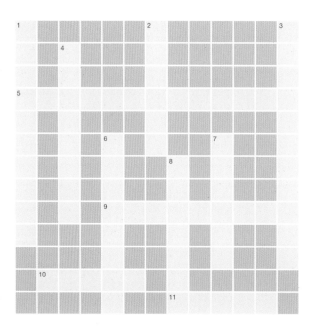

Across

5. something that causes problems or difficulties

9. We have some seats _____ in the front of the cabin.

10. vacant, containing nothing

11. I'll _____ you to your seats.

Down

1. I'm sorry but I'm afraid there was a mistake with the seating

_____.

2. Hold on a _____.

3. I'll check it for you _____.

4. All the seats are _____.

6. being apart

7. I'm _____ your are in the wrong seat.

8. I'm sorry to have kept you _____.

E : Reading Comprehension

Read the text and answer the questions.

How to choose the best seat

Below are some of the factors to consider when choosing your aircraft seat.

Window or aisle?

Both have advantages. If you like to stretch your legs during

© www.hanol.co.kr

the flight, an aisle seat is good for you. Bear in mind, though, that this may be enforced upon you if the person in the window seat wants to get out of their seat. If you prefer to be undisturbed, then the window seat is probably best.

© www.hanol.co.kr

Middle seats are to be avoided

So in a 3-4-3 configuration, typically designated A, B, C, then D, E, F, G and then H, J, K (I is omitted to avoid confusion), the set to avoid are B, E, F and J.

Day flight or night flight?

On a night flight, window seats are preferred by many. You can sleep without being disturbed by anyone wanting access to the aisle, and in economy seats there's the possibility of resting a pillow or rolled up item of clothing against the side of the aircraft to prevent head lolling.

Avoid seats close to the galley

For a day flight being here may be an advantage, since you can receive service more easily, or in premium cabins, perhaps serve yourself. But on night flights the noise can be a nuisance.

Seats by emergency exits are to be preferred

These give more leg room, though they do come with restrictions, most notably that you are able bodied and so can assist in case of emergencies, and of course you cannot stow your luggage under the seat in front of you. Bear in mind also that these are often close to the galley, and so can be noisy.

www.seatplans.com

1. What are the advantages and disadvantages for window and aisle seats?

2. What are the responsibilities of passengers seating in exit seats?

4 Ground service

A : Words

✿ Match the words to the meanings.

> valuables   available   bassinet   return   coatroom   armrest

1. _____ : personal articles of considerable value

2. _____ : ready for use

3. _____ : to go or come back to a former place or condition

4. _____ : a support for the arm at the side of a chair or sofa

5. _____ : a room where coats and other personal belongings can be left

6. _____ : a small basket used for a baby's cradle

✿ Complete the sentences with the correct word or words.

1. Please make sure that your seatbacks are _____ed to the upright position.

2. May I reserve the two front seats which can set up a baby
   _____?

3. I ask you if you know where the _____ is.

4. I'd like to put my _____ in a safe place.

5. I'm sorry but the item is not _____ at this moment.

B : Useful Phrases

1. Would you like

| something to drink? |
| something to read? |
| to read a newspaper? |
| to have a bassinet for your baby? |
| a headset? |
| a blanket? |
| a New York Times, instead? |

2. Here's your

| headphone. |
| newspaper. |
| drink. |

3. I'll get you

| one | now. |
| another one | right away. |

4. If you need anything, please let us know.

Please feel free to ask me if you need any help.

Don't hesitate to ask us if you need help.

C : Conversation

1. Listen to the dialogues below and then practice them with your partner. (C: cabin crew / P: passenger)

Dialogue 1 (Newspaper Service)

C : Would you like to read a newspaper?

P : I'll have the Donga daily.

C : Sure. Here you are.

© www.hanol.co.kr

Dialogue 2 (Newspaper Service)

P : Excuse me, could I have the Washington Post?

C : I'm sorry, sir.
The Washington Post is not available on this flight.
Would you like a New York Times, instead?

P : That will be fine.

C : Here you are.

Dialogue 3 (Headphone Service)

C : Here's your headphone, ma'am.

P : Thank you. Where can I plug in?

C : Right here, on the armrest.

P : Thank you.

C : My pleasure. Please feel free to ask me if you need any help.

P : Okay, I will.

Dialogue 4 (Headphone Service)

P : Excuse me. Something's wrong with my headphone.
I can't hear anything.

C : Oh, I am very sorry. I'll get you another one right away.

P : Okay.

C : Thank you for waiting. Here's your new headphone.
I'm sorry for the inconvenience.

P : That's okay. Thank you.

Dialogue 5 (Blanket and Pillow Service)

P : Can I have one more blanket and pillow?

C : Certainly, ma'am. I'll be back with them right away.

P : Thank you.

C : Here are your blanket and pillow.
Is there anything else I can get for you ma'am?

P : No, thank you.

C : Have a wonderful flight.

Dialogue 6 (Handling coat)

P : Excuse me. Can you keep my coat in the coatroom?

C : Certainly, ma'am. Do you have any valuables in your coat?

P : Oh, I'll take my cell phone out.

C : Sure. I'll return it before landing.

P : Thank you.

C : You're welcome.

Dialogue 7 (Special meal check)

C : Excuse me. Are you Mr. Johnson?

P : Yes, I am.

C : Did you request a vegetarian meal?

P : Yes, I did.

C : All right. I'll serve you a vegetarian meal after take-off.

P : Thank you.

C : You're welcome.

Dialogue 8 (Passenger with a baby)

C : Good morning, ma'am. I'm in charge of this section.
　　We have some baby items such as diapers, baby food, baby
　　formula and bottles.
　　If you need anything, just let me know.

P : All right.

C : Would you like to have a bassinet for your baby?

P : Yes, please.

C : Then I'll set up a bassinet after take-off.
　　And here's a plastic bag for the garbage during the flight.

P : Thank you so much.

C : It's my pleasure, ma'am. Enjoy your flight.

2. Pair Work

Imagine that you and your partner are a member of the cabin crew and a passenger. Use the expressions provided above and continue the conversation by taking turns.

Passenger

1. Ask if there is an American newspaper on board.

2. Ask for an extra blanket and pillow.

Cabin crew

1. Tell the passenger you don't have that newspaper and offer alternatives instead.

2. Tell the passenger you will bring them now. Ask if the passenger needs anything else.

D: Build up

Fill in the blank with a right word from the box below.

| valuables   set up   return   instead   inconvenience   request |

1. Did you _____ a vegetarian meal?

2. I'll _____ a bassinet after take-off.

3. I'll _____ it before landing.

4. Do you have any _____ in your coat?

5. I'm sorry for the _____.

6. Would you like a New York Times, _____?

✿ Match each question with the appropriate answer.

1. Can you keep my coat in the coatroom? •   • Yes, I did.

2. Did you request a vegetarian meal? •   • Certainly. Do you
                                                     have any valuables
                                                     in your coat?

3. Can I have the Washington Post?   •   • Yes, sir. I'll bring
                                                     them for you right
                                                     away.

4. Can I have one more blanket and pillow? •   • Sure, here it is.

✿ Unscramble the words to make sentences.

1. like to have   Would you   for your baby?   a bassinet

   ⇨ _____

2. just   If you   let me know.   need anything,

   ⇨ _____

3. anything   for you   Is there   I can do   ma'am?

   ⇨ _____

4. right away.   I'll   another one   get you

   ⇨ _____

5. on this flight.   The Washington Post   available   is not

⇨ _____

6. like to   Would you   a newspaper?   read

⇨ _____

Complete the crossword puzzle below.

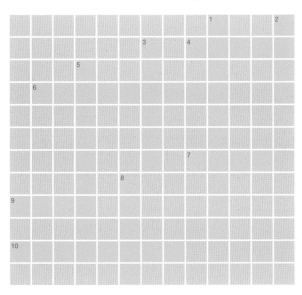

Across

4. I'll _____ you your special meal after take-off.

6. ready for use

7. Please feel _____ to ask me if you need any help.

9. the food you eat as breakfast, lunch, or dinner

10. a small basket used for a baby's cradle

Down

1. someone who never eats meat or fish

2. _____ is your headphone.

3. I'm in _____ of this section.

5. personal articles of considerable value

8. I'll _____ it to you right now.

E : Reading Comprehension

Read the text and answer the questions.

Special meals on board

Do you prefer a vegetarian, kosher, muslim or hindu meal on board? Or do you prefer a lactose intolerant, gluten intolerant or fat free meal? For intercontinental flights you can order a variety of special meals.

Order your special meal

Special meals are free of charge and served exclusively on intercontinental flights. Make sure to order until 24 hours (Kosher meals: until 48 hours) before departure. Ordering is easy on KLM. com. Simply select your preference when booking.

Children's meals

- Baby meal: we recommend always bringing your baby's food yourself. Any restrictions at the airport on bringing liquids do not apply to baby food. On intercontinental flights, we have only a limited number of sterilized meals available.
- Child meal: for intercontinental flights you can order a child meal free of charge. It is packed in a colorful box.

Vegetarian meals

- Vegetarian meal: this meal does not contain any meat, meat products or seafood, but may contain dairy products, eggs and vegetables.
- Asian vegetarian meal: spicy vegetarian combinations which may contain a limited amount of dairy products.
- Vegetarian vegan meal: no animal products, eggs or dairy products.

Medical diets

- Diabetic meal: meal containing a balance of complex carbohydrates, proteins, healthy fats and low sugar content.
- Low fat meal: this meal does not contain more than 3 grams of total fat per 100 grams food.
- Low salt meal: this meal does not contain highly salted ingredients and no salt is added.
- Gluten intolerant meal: ingredients are verified to ensure gluten is not present.
- Lactose intolerant meal: dairy products are omitted.

Religious meal preferences

- Muslim meal: this meal does not contain pork, pork by-products or food containing alcohol. If this meal contains meat, it comes from ritually slaughtered animals.
- Kosher meal: for this meal, the food is chosen, prepared and served in accordance with Jewish dietary laws and customs.
- Hindu meal: this meal does not contain beef, veal, pork or derived products from these types of meat.

www.klm.com

1. When should the special meal be ordered?

2. Decide whether the statements are true or false.

1) On intercontinental flights, they have many different types of sterilized meals for babies. (   )

2) Hindu meal does not contain beef, veal, and pork. (   )

3) Vegetarian vegan meal contains eggs or dairy products. (   )

4) For the kosher meal, the food is chosen, prepared and served according to Jewish dietary laws and customs. (   )

Preparing for take-off

Words

⚙ Match the words to the meanings.

take off	seatbelt	fasten	upright
seatback	safety	electronic devices	

1. _____ : close something by means of a strap

2. _____ : the part of a chair that supports the back

3. _____ : the vertical as in position

4. _____ : to leave the ground and begin to fly

5. _____ : the state of being safe

6. _____ : items such as televisions, computers, and cell phones

7. _____ : a belt that fastens around you in a vehicle to keep safely secured

⚙ Complete the sentences with the correct word or words.

1. Fly with an airline which offers _____ TV screens.

2. _____ is a primary consideration at such events.

3. The airplane could not _____ due to bad weather.

4. Using non-approved portable _____ is strictly prohibited in the cabin.

5. Why do we put seats _____ in an airplane?

6. _____ the seatbelt to make sure it is not loose to protect your body.

B: Useful Phrases

1. Would you please | fasten your seatbelt?
   | close your tray table?
   | open your window shades?
   | return your seatback to the upright position?
   | hold your baby outside of your seatbelt?

2. Would you mind | fastening your seatbelt, | please?
   | closing your tray table,
   | opening your window shades,
   | returning your seatback to the upright position,
   | holding your baby outside of your seatbelt,

3. We'll be taking off   shortly.

                             soon.

                             in a minute.

C : Conversation

1. Listen to the dialogues below and then practice them with your partner. (C: cabin crew / P: passenger)

Dialogue 1 (Safety check - seatbelt/seatback)

C : Would you please fasten your seatbelt?
    We'll be taking off shortly.

P : Sure.

C : And return your seatback to the upright position, please.

P : Oh, okay.

C : Thank you, sir.

Dialogue 2 (Safety check - showing how to fasten seatbelts)

P : Excuse me, will you show me how to fasten my seatbelt?

C : Sure, ma'am. Pull it this way and insert the link into the buckle.

P : Oh, thank you.

C : You're welcome. If you need any help, just push this call button.

P : Alright. Thanks.

Dialogue 3 (Safety check - tray table)

C : Excuse me, sir. Would you mind closing your tray table, please?

P : Alright.

C : Thank you. You can use it again after take-off.

P : Okay.

Dialogue 4 (Safety check – baby's seatbelt)

C : Excuse me, ma'am.
Would you please hold your baby outside of your seatbelt?

P : Do I have to?

C : Yes, ma'am.
It will be more comfortable and safer for both of you.

P : Okay, I see.

Dialogue 5 (Safety check - window shades)

C : Excuse me, could you please open your window shades?

P : Oh, the sun is too bright for me.

C : I'm sorry but for safety reasons, we have to keep them open during take-off and landing.

P : Okay.

C : Thank you for your cooperation.

Dialogue 6 (Safety check –electronic devices)

C : Excuse me, sir. Is your cell phone set to flight mode?

P : I don't think so.

C : You are allowed to use your electronic devices during the flight as long as they are set to flight mode.

P : Okay, I will.

C : Thank you for your cooperation.

© www.hanol.co.kr

2. Pair Work

Imagine that you and your partner are a member of the cabin crew and a passenger. Use the expressions provided above and continue the conversation by taking turns.

Passenger

1. Ask how to fasten your seatbelt.

2. Cooperate with what the cabin crew says.

Cabin crew

1. Politely explain to the passenger how to fasten a seatbelt.

2. Ask the passenger to fasten his or her seatbelt, return their seatback to the upright position, close the tray table, open the window shade, and switch the cell phone to flight mode.

D : Build up

 Fill in the blank with a right word from the box below.

| call button   seatbelt   taking off   comfortable   closing |

1. Would you please fasten your _____?

2. Would you mind _____ your tray table?

3. We'll be _____ shortly.

4. If you need any help, just push this _____.

5. It will be more _____ for both of you.

✿ Unscramble the words to make sentences.

1. upright position.   Please return   to the   your seatback

   ⇨ _____

2. your baby   please   outside of   hold   Would you   your seatbelt?

   ⇨ _____

3. show me   Will you   how to   my seatbelt?   fasten

   ⇨ _____

4. after   You can   again   use it   take-off.

   ⇨ _____

Complete the crossword puzzle below.

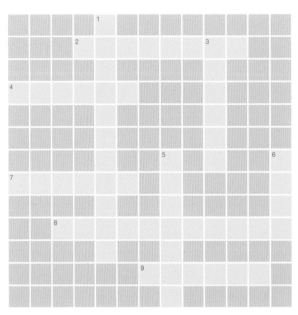

Across

2. to leave the ground and begin to fly

4. Pull the seatbelt this way and insert the link into the _____.

7. Please direct your attention to the video screens for _____ information.

8. Thank you for your _____.

9. You are allowed to use your cell phone as long as they are set to _____ mode.

Down

1. If you need any help, just push this _____.

3. close something by means of a strap

5. We'll be departing _____.

6. We have to keep the window shade _____ during take-off
    and landing

E : Reading Comprehension

🌸 Read the text and answer the questions.

In-flight Safety Regulation

Whenever the "FASTEN
SEAT BELT" sign is activated,
please return to your seat and
fasten your seat belt securely.
Upon takeoff and landing,
please put away your tray table
and return your seat back to
the upright position. Besides,
as turbulence often comes
unexpectedly, we suggest all

passengers fasten seat belts while being seated and review the safety
instruction in the seat pocket.

Blankets are served to passengers on some of our flights for passengers' comfort. Please fasten your seat belt outside the blanket. This is to make your seat belt visible to cabin crew, who can make sure your seat belt is duly fastened.

After landing it takes time for aircraft taxi to parking bay. The time varies at different airports. Please remain seated until the "FASTEN SEAT BELT" sign is turned off by captain.

www.mandarin-airlines.com

1. When the seatbelt sign is on, what do you have to do?

2. List at least three things to do during take-off and landing.

In-flight Service

In-flight Service

이륙 후 승무원의 업무

1) 좌석벨트 상시 착용 안내 방송

기내 방송 담당 승무원은 Seatbelt sign이 꺼지면 좌석벨트 상시 착용 안내 방송을 실시한다.

2) 식음료 서비스

• Disposable towel 또는 Cotton towel을 서비스한다.

- 식전 음료(Aperitif)를 서비스한다. 항공사, 출발시간, 비행시간, 식사 시간대 등에 따라 서비스 방법에 차이가 있으나, 대개 Tray 또는 음료 Cart를 이용하여 서비스한다.
- Meal tray를 제공한다. 식사 시간대에 따라 와인이나 Hot beverage를 함께 서비스한다.
- 물과 와인을 Refill하고 Hot beverage를 서비스한다.
- Meal tray를 회수한다.

3) 입국 서류 배포 및 작성 협조

승무원은 기내식 서비스 후 해당 도착지에 맞게 입국서류를 배포하고 작성을 도와드린다.

4) 면세품 판매

면세품 판매를 알리는 기내 방송을 실시한 뒤, 판매 담당 승무원들은 Cart에 면세품을 준비하여 객실을 순회하며 구매를 원하는 승객에게 면세품을 판매한다.

Beverage and Meal service

A : Words

Match the words to the meanings.

| apology | recommend | on the rocks | kosher meal |
| selection | entrée | liqueur |

1. _____ : to suggest that someone or something would be good

2. _____ : to have an alcoholic drink with pieces of ice

3. _____ : a range of different types of something

4. _____ : an act of saying that you are sorry for something

5. _____ : food that meets the requirements of Jewish law

6. _____ : strong and sweet liquor usually served after a meal

7. _____ : the main dish of a meal

☼ Complete the sentences with the correct word or words.

1. You have a choice of _____ today; chicken or fish.

2. I'd like a vodka _____.

3. We _____ that you keep your seatbelt fastened at all times.

4. Please accept my sincere _____.

5. The duty free shop stock a _____ of exclusive travel items.

B : Useful Phrases

1. Would you	like	something to drink?
		something to eat?
		a cup of coffee?
	care for	some more?
		another drink?
		something else?

2. How would you like your	coffee?
	vodka?
	whisky?
	steak?

3. I'm afraid we've run out of the beef.
   chicken.
   fish.

4. (I hope you) Enjoy your drink.
   meal.

5. Did you enjoy your drink?
   meal?

6. Are you finished with your towel?
   done drink?
   meal?

7. May I take your towel?
   cup?
   tray?

C : Conversation

1. Listen to the dialogues below and then practice them with your partner. (C: cabin crew / P: passenger)

Dialogue 1 (Towel Service)

C : Would you like to use a hot towel, sir?

P : Yes, please.

C : It's very hot. Please be careful.

P : Thank you.

......

C : Excuse me, are you finished with your towel?

P : Yes, thank you.

C : (taking towel) You're welcome.

Dialogue 2 (Drink service)

C : Would you like something to drink?

P : What do you have?

C : We have juices, soft drinks, beers, coffee and tea.

P : I'll have tomato juice.

C : Sure, ma'am. Here is your tomato juice. Enjoy your drink.

Dialogue 3 (Coffee service)

C : Would you care for something to drink?

P : I'd like to have a cup of coffee.

C : How would you like your coffee?

P : With cream, please.

C : Certainly, sir. Here's your coffee with cream. It's hot.
     Please be careful.

Dialogue 4 (Beer service)

C : What would you like to drink?

P : I'll have a Heineken, please.

C : I am sorry but I'm afraid we don't have a Heineken on this
flight.

P : Then what kind of beer do you have?

C : We have a selection of Budweiser, Miller, Cass, and Hite.

P : Budweiser, please.

C : Certainly, ma'am. Here's your beer. Enjoy your drink.

Dialogue 5 (Whisky service)

C : Would you care for something to drink?

P : Can I have a glass of whisky?

C : Sure, how would you like your whisky?

P : On the rocks, please.

C : Yes, sir. Here is your whisky on the rocks. Enjoy your drink.

P : Thank you.

Dialogue 6 (Cocktail service)

C : Can I get you something to drink before dinner?

P : Yes, I'll have Tequila Sunrise.

C : I'm very sorry. But we don't have Tequila on board.
   Would you like something else?

P : What do you recommend?

C : May I suggest you try the Screwdriver?
   It's made of vodka and orange juice.

P : I'll try that.

C : Just a moment, please. ... Here's your Screwdriver.
   I hope you enjoy it.

P : (after drinking) Hmm, I think it's a bit strong.

C : Oh, I'm very sorry.
   May I add some more orange juice?

P : Yes, please.

C : Here you are. How is it now?

P : It tastes much better.
   Thank you.

C : My pleasure, sir.
   Enjoy your drink.

Dialogue 7 (Cocktail service)

C : Would you like something to drink?

P : Yes, can I have a Black Russian?

C : I'm sorry but I'm afraid I don't know how it's made.

P : It is made of vodka and coffee liqueur.

C : Alright. I'll try my best. … Here you are. I hope you enjoy it.

P : It tastes great. Thank you.

C : I'm very happy that you like it.
    May I get you some more peanuts?

P : That would be good.

C : Here you are. Enjoy your drink.

Dialogue 8 (Spilled drink on a passenger)

C : I'm terribly sorry, sir. Let me get something to wipe it up.
...May I help you wipe it up?

P : No, that's fine. I can manage it.

C : Please accept my apology.

P : That's okay. Never mind.

C : I am sorry again, sir.

© www.hanol.co.kr

Dialogue 9 (Drink refill)

C : Would you care for another drink?

P : Sure. I'd like a glass of red wine, please.

C : Here is your red wine. Enjoy your drink.

Dialogue 10 (Empty cup collecting)

C : Excuse me. Are you finished with your drink?

P : Yes, I'm done.

C : May I take your cup?

P : Yes, please. Thank you.

C : You're welcome.

Dialogue 11 (Meal service: short-haul flight)

C : Excuse me, we're serving lunch now.
   Would you please open your tray table?

P : Sure. What do you have?

C : We have Chinese style chicken with noodles today.

P : Do you have anything else?

C : I'm sorry but I'm afraid we only
   offer one choice of meal for
   the short-haul flight.

P : Okay.

C : Here you are. I hope you
   enjoy your meal.

Dialogue 12 (Meal service: medium and long-haul flight)

C : Ma'am. We're serving dinner now.
We have beef with potatoes and fish with vegetables.
Which one do you prefer?

P : I'll have fish with vegetables.

C : Would you like to open your tray
table? Here's your meal.
Would you care for some wine
with your meal?

P : White wine, please.

C : Here you go. Enjoy your meal.

Dialogue 13 (Meal service: medium and long-haul flight)

C : We have a selection of Bibimbop, chicken curry, and Japanese
style seafood. Which one would you like?

P : What's Bibimbop?

C : It's a Korean traditional dish. It is served with
a bowl of warm rice topped with assorted
vegetables. You can enjoy it after mixing
with chili pepper paste.

P : Sounds good. I'll try that one.

C : Here's your Bibimbop. I hope you enjoy your meal.

Dialogue 14 (Meal service: Entrée run out.)

C : Excuse me, ma'am. We had a choice of beef and chicken
    but I'm afraid we've run out of the beef today.
    We only have chicken left. Would that be alright with you?

P : Alright. I'll take it.

C : Thank you for your understanding.
    I hope you enjoy your meal.

Dialogue 15 (Special meal service)

C : Excuse me, sir. Are you Mr. James Baker?

P : Yes, I am.

C : Did you request a kosher meal?

P : Yes, I did.

C : This is the kosher meal you requested.
    May I open and heat it up for
    you?

P : Yes, please.

C : It will take about 20 minutes.
    Please wait for a while.

Dialogue 16 (Hot beverage service after meal service)

C : Would you care for some coffee?

P : Yes, please.

C : Could you please put your cup on this tray? … Thank you.
Here's your coffee.
It's very hot. Please be careful.
Would you like some cream and sugar with your coffee?

P : No, thanks.

C : Enjoy your coffee.

Dialogue 17 (Meal tray collecting)

C : Excuse me. Did you enjoy your meal?
(Are you finished with your meal?)

P : Yes, I did. (Yes, I am.)

C : Thanks. May I take your tray?

P : Yes, please.

C : Thank you.

2. Pair Work

Imagine that you and your partner are a member of the cabin crew and a passenger. Use the expressions provided above and continue the conversation by taking turns.

Cabin crew

1. Take a drink order and offer it to the passenger.
   Explain what you have for meals.
   Serve the passengers what they want.

2. Ask whether they enjoyed the meal or not.
   Collect the meal tray.

Passenger

1. Ask for a drink.
   Ask about the meal options.
   Choose what you like.

2. Tell the cabin crew whether you liked it or not.

D: Build up

Fill in the blank with a right word from the box below.

| wipe | understanding | afraid | apology | kosher meal |

1. Did you request a _____ ?

2. Thank you for your _____ .

3. Please accept my _____ .

4. I am sorry but I'm _____ we don't have a Heineken on this flight.

5. Let me get something to _____ it up.

Match each question with the appropriate answer.

1. Did you enjoy your meal?   •   • I'll have beef.

2. May I open and heat it up for you? •   • Yes, I did.

3. Which one do you prefer?   •   • Yes, please.

4. Are you finished with your drink? •   • Not yet.

5. How would you like your whisky? •   • On the rocks, please.

Unscramble the words to make sentences.

1. now.   We're   lunch   serving

   ⇨ _____

2. you   Would   table?   please   open   tray   your

   ⇨ _____

3. for   drink?   Would   care   another   you

⇨ _____

4. but I'm afraid   how it's made.   I'm sorry   I don't know

⇨ _____

5. juice.   It's   of   and   made   orange   vodka

⇨ _____

✿ Complete the crossword puzzle below.

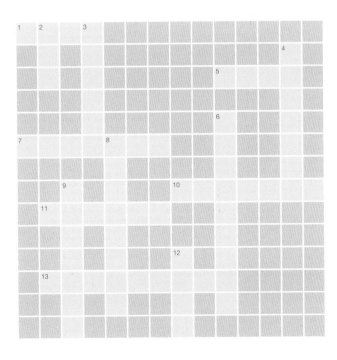

Across

1. Would you _____ for something to drink?

5. It's _____ of vodka and orange juice.

7. It's very hot. Please be _____.

10. an act of saying that you are sorry for something

11. You can enjoy it after _____ with chili pepper paste.

13. a range of different types of something

Down

2. May I _____ some more orange juice?

3. the main dish of a meal

4. We're _____ dinner now.

6. to suggest that someone or something would be good

8. Are you _____ with your drink?

9. strong and sweet liquor usually served after a meal

12. Let me get something to _____ it up.

E : Reading Comprehension

Read the text and answer the questions.

Dining in Economy class

In KLM Economy Class, you can enjoy a broad selection of beverages, a Tasty Blue meal or a hearty sandwich.

Economy Class intercontinental

On all KLM intercontinental flights, we welcome you on board with a beverage of choice. Before every meal you receive a nice hot towel for refreshment and an aperitif with nuts. You are then served an hors-d'oeuvre, your choice of one of our two Tasty Blue hot meals and a dessert. With your meal you naturally get a fresh bread roll with butter and cheese. After dinner, we offer complimentary coffee, tea or a liqueur.

On shorter flights, we serve a fresh sandwich or other snack before landing. On longer flights, we serve a second meal. Depending on the time of day this will be breakfast, lunch or dinner. Between meals, we serve you snacks, ice cream or a sandwich. When you would like some more, you can ask the crew for a sweet or savory snack.

Beverages

We serve hot and cold drinks (alcoholic and non-alcoholic), including sustainable coffee and tea, soft drinks, fruit juice, beer and specially blended and award-winning wine, together with your meal. Throughout the entire flight, we offer something to drink once every hour.

A la carte menu

On most KLM intercontinental flights departing from Amsterdam, you have an even larger selection of hot meals to choose from when you order an à la carte meal at KLM.com before your flight.

To and from Asia

On all KLM flights to and from China, India, Japan and Korea, we offer Asian meals prepared by renowned restaurants.

www.klm.com

1. What do you receive before every meal?

2. What can you get between meals?

3. Decide whether the statements are true or false.

    1) They serve light meals such as a sandwich or snack on short-
       haul flight. (   )

    2) Hot beverages are not free of charge. (   )

    3) They offer Asian cuisine on all flights to and from Amsterdam.
       (   )

2 In-flight sales

A : Words

✿ Match the words to the meanings.

| accept | duty free | purchase | allowance | change | liquor | receipt |

1. _____ : free of tax

2. _____ : an alcoholic drink such as whisky, gin, vodka, and brandy

3. _____ : to acquire something by paying for it

4. _____ : to receive

5. _____ : money received as the balance of the sum paid for something

6. _____ : a piece of paper proving that something has been paid for

7. _____ : the amount that is permitted

✿ Complete the sentences with the correct word or words.

1. You are entitled to $600 in _____ items.

2. Don't forget to sign the _____.

3. You may _____ duty free items now, or order items for your return flight.

4. The duty free allowance for Korea is 1 bottle of _____ and 1 carton of cigarettes.

B ⋮ Useful Phrases

1. | Would you like to | buy | any duty free items? |
   |---|---|---|
   | Do you want to | purchase | |
   | | order | |

2. I'm sorry but I'm afraid

we've run out of _____ today.
_____ is all sold out now.
we do not accept _____.
it is not available since we are
preparing for landing.
I don't have enough change now.

3. It costs _____ US dollars.
    The total comes to _____ US dollars.
    Your items are _____ dollars in total.
    Your change comes to _____ dollars.

4. Here is your   change.
                   receipt.

C : Conversation

1. Listen to the dialogues below and then practice them with your
    partner. (C: cabin crew / P: passenger)

Dialogue 1 (In-flight shopping guide)

C : Would you like to buy any duty free items?

P : What kind of items do you have?

C : We have cosmetics, perfumes, liquors and gift items.
    Here's your in-flight duty free magazine.
    It has all the information about our duty free items.
    Please take your time to look at it and let us know.

P : Okay, thanks.

Dialogue 2 (Duty free allowance)

C : Excuse me, sir.
  Would you like to purchase any duty free items?

P : I need some whisky.
  How many bottles of whisky can I take into the USA?

C : You're allowed to take 1 liter of liquor.

P : Then bring me one bottle of Johnnie Walker Blue.

C : Certainly, sir. Here you are. How would you like to pay?

P : I'll pay in US dollars.

C : It costs 164 US dollars.

P : Here's 200 dollars.

C : Thank you. Here is your change, 36 dollars.

Dialogue 3 (Items sold out/ Unacceptable currency)

P : I'd like to buy two boxes of Hawaiian Sun chocolate.

C : I'm sorry but I'm afraid we've run out of Hawaiian Sun chocolate.
Would you like something else, instead?
We have Godiva, Lindt, and Royce chocolate.

P : Then I'll take two boxes of Godiva chocolate.
Can I pay in Canadian dollars?

C : I'm sorry but I'm afraid we do not accept Canadian dollars.

P : Can I pay by credit card, then?

C : Certainly, ma'am. That will be 56 US dollars.

P : Here's my credit card.

C : Could I have your signature, please?

P : Sure.

C : Here's your receipt. Thank you, ma'am.

Dialogue 4 (Change unavailable)

P : How much are these?

C : The total comes to 241 US dollars.

P : Here's 300 dollars.

C : I'm sorry but I'm afraid I don't have enough change now.
I'll bring your change as soon as possible.
Would that be alright?

P : No problem.

C : … I'm very sorry to have kept you waiting.
Here's your change, 59 dollars.
Is that correct?

P : Yes, it is. Thanks.

C : You're welcome, sir.

© www.hanol.co.kr

Dialogue 5 (Refund)

P : Excuse me. Can I get a refund on these cosmetics?

C : Sure. Let me have the receipt, please.

P : Here you go.

C : Thank you. Just a moment, please.

    … May I have the cosmetics?

    Here's your refund receipt, ma'am.

P : Thank you.

C : You're welcome.

Dialogue 6 (Sales unavailable due to preparation for landing)

P : Excuse me. Can I buy some duty free items now?

C : I'm sorry but I'm afraid it is not available since we are
    preparing for landing.

P : Oh, I see.

C : Thank you for your understanding.

2. Pair Work

Imagine that you and your partner are a member of the cabin crew and a passenger. Use the expressions provided above and continue the conversation by taking turns.

Passenger

1. Try to buy duty-free items.

2. Ask about the duty-free allowance.
   Pay for the items with your credit card.

Cabin crew

1. Give information about duty-free items. Explain why the item is unavailable and recommend similar ones.

2. Explain about duty-free restrictions. Provide information about the payment methods.

D : Build up

❀ Fill in the blank with a right word from the box below.

| information | allowed | run out of | change | accept |

1. It has all the _____ about our duty free items.

2. You're _____ to take 1 liter of liquor.

3. I'm sorry but I'm afraid we've _____ Hawaiian Sun chocolate today.

4. I'm sorry but I'm afraid I don't have enough _____ now.

5. I'm sorry but I'm afraid we do not _____ Canadian dollars.

❀ Match each question with the appropriate answer.

1. Would you like to buy any duty free •   • Certainly, ma'am.
   items?

2. How would you like to pay?   •   • I need some whisky.

3. Can I buy some duty free items now? •   • I'll pay by credit card.
   (While preparing for landing)

4. Can I get a refund on these   •   • It is not available
   cosmetics?   since we are preparing
                                                 for landing.

Unscramble the words to make sentences.

1. instead? you Would something like else,

2. have please? Could signature, your I

3. dollars. The to 100 total US comes

4. to have kept I'm you waiting. very sorry

5. not available I'm afraid are preparing since we for landing. it is

6. understanding. you Thank your for

Complete the crossword puzzle below.

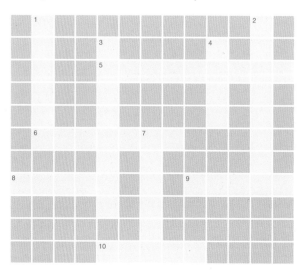

Across

5. The duty free _____ for Korea is 1 bottle of liquor and 1 carton of cigarettes.

6. There is a duty free item _____ in the back of the cabin.

8. You can _____ to the in-flight magazine in your seat pocket.

9. Please let me know when you are ready to _____ some duty free items.

10. Your items are 112 dollars in _____.

Down

1. Can I get a _____ on these items?

2. What is the _____ rate today?

3. Write your name and _____ number on the back.

4. I'll pay with _____ .

7. We_____ Korean won, U.S. dollars, and Japanese yen.

E : Reading Comprehension

✿ Read the text and answer the questions.

In-flight Sales

Indulge in some retail therapy with Qatar Airways extensive in-flight shopping selection

Choose from an exclusive collection of the best-selling duty free products from the comfort of your seat. Browse through our in-flight duty free magazine, Shopping Extravaganza, and choose from our collection of fragrances, cosmetics, skincare, watches, jewellery, fashion accessories, toys, and Qatar Airways memorabilia. Updated every 6 months, Shopping Extravaganza offers an ideal balance of classic best sellers and contemporary new launches.

Qatar Airways In-Flight Duty Free accepts all major currencies and credit cards.

Shop onboard

Our in-flight duty free magazine, Shopping Extravaganza is available onboard to browse through and help you with your selection. Find a last-minute gift for a loved one or a product to pamper yourself with—whatever you choose, it's sure to be special.

Shopping Extravaganza

In-flight Duty Free
Magazine Issue No. 38

www.qatarairways.com

1. What is the name of the in-flight duty free magazine of Qatar Airways?

2. Decide whether the statements are true or false.

   1) The in-flight duty free magazine is updated every month.

      (   )

   2) Qatar Airways In-Flight Duty Free accepts all major currencies

      and credit cards. (   )

Handling complaints and requests

 **Words**

✿ Match the words to the meanings.

aviation law temperature assistance lavatory pressure cooperation

1. _____ : the degree of how hot or cold of a body or
   environment

2. _____ : force exerted on a surface by pressing it

3. _____ : an act of working together

4. _____ : an act of help

5. _____ : a room equipped with a toilet and sink

6. _____ : the law that concerns flight and air travel

✿ Complete the sentences with the correct word or words.

1. Disturbing cabin crew is strictly prohibited according to the _____.

2. Smoking in the cabin or in the _____ is not allowed during the flight.

3. The discomfort some passengers feel on airplanes could be due to the air _____.

4. Cabin crew will offer _____ to passengers with disabilities.

B : Useful Phrases

1. I'm so sorry   for the inconvenience.
   to have kept you waiting.
   to keep you waiting.

2. Is there anything I can do for you?
   What can I do for you?
   If you need any assistance, please let us know.

3. Please accept our apology.

I'm very sorry to make you unpleasant.

4. I have to inform you that smoking is against the law.

By the aviation law, smoking is not permitted on board.

5. Let me get you another meal right away.

I'll bring you a new one right away.

C : Conversation

1. Listen to the dialogues below and then practice them with your partner. (C: cabin crew / P: passenger)

Dialogue 1 (Cabin temperature)

P : Excuse me. I think it is very cold in here.

C : I'm so sorry. I'll check the cabin temperature first and get you a blanket. Would you like something hot to drink?

P : Yes, please. Can I have some green tea, please?

C : Sure. Just a moment, please.

   (After a while) Here's a blanket and a cup of green tea.

P : Thank you.

C : I'm afraid it takes some time for adjusting the temperature.

P : That's okay. Thank you.

Dialogue 2 (A drunken passenger wants more liquor.)

P : Excuse me. I want some more whisky.

C : I am sorry but I am afraid you've already had three glasses of whisky. Would you care for a non-alcoholic drink instead?

P : No, I want to drink whisky.

C : Due to cabin pressure, when drinking the same amount of alcohol, you are more drunk in the air than on the ground.

P : Okay, okay. Give me some ice water, then.

C : Certainly, sir. Thank you for your understanding.

Dialogue 3 (Unruly children)

P1 : Excuse me. I want to get some sleep, but those children are making so much noise.
Could you please say something to them?

C : I'm so sorry for the inconvenience. I'll see what I can do. (goes to their parent) Excuse me, ma'am. I'm sorry but some of the passengers would like to take a rest.
Could you please keep the kids a little quieter?

P2 : Oh, I see. I'm sorry.

C : Thank you for your cooperation.

© www.hanol.co.kr

Dialogue 4 (Crying babies)

C : Excuse me. Is there anything I can do for you, ma'am?

P : I don't know why she doesn't stop crying.

C : Well, it's hard for babies to travel long distance. If she might have sore ears, breastfeeding or bottle-feeding your baby will help to ease any painful ear popping.

P : Oh, I see.

C : If you need any assistance, please let us know.
We'll be glad to help.

Dialogue 5 (Smoking in the lavatory)

C : Excuse me. Please put out your cigarette and come out of the lavatory.

P : Is something wrong?

C : Sir, by the aviation law, smoking is not permitted on board, including in the lavatories.

P : Okay, okay.

C : Once again I have to inform you that smoking is against the law and will be reported to the captain and the airport police.

P : I see. I won't smoke again. I'm sorry.

C : Thank you for your cooperation.

Dialogue 6 (Lukewarm meal)

P : Excuse me. My meal is not hot enough.

C : I'm really sorry. I'll heat it up for you immediately.
Would you like some bread while you are waiting?

P : Yes, please.

C : Here is your bread. Just a moment, please.
(After a while) I'm sorry to have kept you waiting. Here's your
meal. I hope it is hot enough this time. How is it?

P : Good. Thank you.

Dialogue 7 (Foreign object in the meal)

P : Excuse me. There's something strange in my food.
You can't expect me to eat this.

C : I'm terribly sorry. Please let me take your tray and get you another
meal right away.
… Here's another meal. Please accept our apology.
(After collecting the meal tray)
I'm very sorry to make you unpleasant today. I'll file a report
and send the object to the catering center to ensure that this
thing won't happen again.

Dialogue 8 (Special meal not loaded)

C : Excuse me. We have beef and chicken for lunch.
Which one would you prefer?

P : Oh, I don't eat meat. So I requested a vegetarian meal when
I made a reservation.

C : I'm very sorry. May I have your name, please?

P : My name is Rachel Kim.

C : Could you please wait for a moment, ma'am?
I'll check on your meal immediately.

P : Okay.

C : I'm terribly sorry, but your meal is not on board the aircraft.
Our ground staff must have made a mistake.
Please accept our apology.

P : That's very disappointing.

C : I'm sorry for the inconvenience.
May I offer you some salad and bread, instead?

P : Well, alright.

C : Thank you. I'll bring them for you right
away.
… Here's your fruits and salad with
bread.
I hope you enjoy your meal.

Dialogue 9 (AVOD system out of order)

P : Excuse me. I think the AVOD system is not working.

C : Is that so? Let me check it, please.

… I'm sorry but I'm afraid I have to reset the system in your seat.

Would you mind waiting for a while?

P : Alright.

C : Thank you. May I get you a newspaper or something to drink?

P : No, thanks.

C : I'm sorry for the inconvenience.

(after a while)

Thank you for waiting, sir. I think it's working properly now.

P : Yes, thank you.

C : My pleasure. If you need anything during the flight, please let me know.

2. Pair Work

Imagine that you and your partner are a member of the cabin crew and a passenger. Use the expressions provided above and continue the conversation by taking turns.

Passenger

1. Ask to adjust the cabin temperature.

2. Ask for some more liquor. You have already had a few glass of liquor.

3. Complain about passengers making so much noise.

Cabin crew

1. Tell the passenger you will check the temperature. Offer an extra blanket or a hot drink.

2. Explain politely how fast they could be more drunk than on the ground. Offer some non-alcoholic drinks instead.

3. Tell the passenger you will ask them to be quiet.

D : Build up

Fill in the blank with a right word from the box below.

| mistake | smoking | temperature | assistance | instead |

1. I'll check the cabin _____ first and get you a blanket for you.

2. I have to inform you that _____ is against the law.

3. If you need any _____ , please let us know.

4. Would you care for a non-alcoholic drink _____?

5. Our ground staff must have made a _____.

✿ Unscramble the words to make sentences.

1. inconvenience.   I'm   the   sorry   so   for

   ⇨ _____

2. heat   I'll   for   immediately.   it   you   up

   ⇨ _____

3. some bread   Would you like   you are waiting?   while

   ⇨ _____

4. away.   I'll   another   get   right   you   meal

   ⇨ _____

5. meal   I'll   your   check   immediately.   on

   ⇨ _____

⚙ Complete the crossword puzzle below.

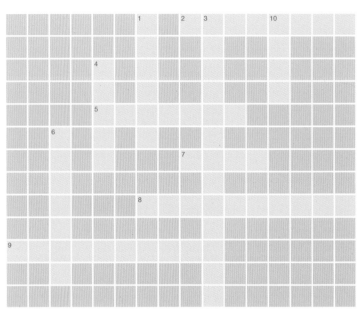

Across

2. He looked too sick to fly on a long _____ flight.

5. _____ is strictly prohibited in an airplane.

7. My _____ is not hot enough.

8. an act of help

9. Would it be possible to request a _____ meal?

Down

1. strong alcoholic drinks

3. We apologize for any _____ caused by the late departure.

4. adjust or set a machine or device

6. Please accept my sincere _____.

10. audio and video on demand

E : Reading Comprehension

⚙ Read the text and answer the questions.

How to Handle Customer Complaints

© www.hanol.co.kr

Customer complaints are inevitable, no matter how streamlined your business. They must always be acknowledged and dealt with effectively. By ignoring or dismissing complaints, you are effectively telling the customer that you don't value their opinions. Many business owners see complaint management as a time-consuming and frustrating process. However, by developing an efficient system, complaints can be resolved quickly and easily.

Here is a step-by-step guide to dealing with dissatisfied customers.

Taking the Complaint

- When a customer first makes a complaint, take a step back. An emotional response will only serve to irritate the customer further.

- Give the customer your full attention and listen to the whole problem before responding. Put yourself in their shoes - if you had a problem, you would want someone to listen to you.

- Don't jump the gun. You might deal with complaints on a regular basis, and may well have handled a similar situation before. However, for the customer, their complaint is unique to them. Treat them as an important individual by listening to their problem in full.

- Try to understand. In the face of a complaint, it's easy to be defensive. - particularly if you don't believe you're at fault. However, you have to put yourself in the customer's shoes. If you were on the receiving end of their experience, would you personally be satisfied?

- Always use your initiative when dealing with complaints. If the blame lies with one particular member of staff, it is often best to remove the customer from their presence. This can defuse tension and emotion, and help the customer to re-evaluate their anger.

- However, never pass the customer around from person to person. Each complaint should ideally be handled by one staff member. Therefore, you should always ensure that the person assigned to the case has the authority to deal with the situation.

Finding a Solution

- Give a sincere apology immediately. Any number of factors could have contributed to the issue, and you might not be at fault. However, you need to take responsibility for the problem. Sometimes, an apology is all it takes to placate an angry customer.

- Customers never want to hear excuses. However, you are fully entitled to briefly explain why they didn't receive the standard of service they expected. This should take place after you've listened to their complaint and made an apology.

• Sometimes, a complaint will be followed by a request for compensation - typically a refund or a voucher. However, customers often haven't planned beyond making the initial complaint. In these cases, ask the customer for their desired outcome. This makes them feel both involved and valued.

www.skillsyouneed.com

1. What would you do when a customer makes a complaint?

2. Decide whether the statements are true or false.

   1) Customer complaints can be resolved by developing an efficient system. (   )

   2) When a customer makes a complaint, try to be defensive as much as you can. (   )

   3) Each complaint should ideally be handled by one staff member. (   )

4 Entry documents

A : Words

✿ Match the words to the meanings.

| transit | arrival card | resident | complete |
| embarkation | visitor | customs form |

1. _____ : a legal document completed by a passenger when entering a certain country

2. _____ : an official document that lists details of goods that the passenger is bringing into a certain country

3. _____ : to write the required information on a form

4. _____ : a person who lives in a certain place on a long-term basis

5. _____ : the act of going onto a ship or aircraft

6. _____ : the act of passing across or through

7. _____ : a person who visits a person or place

✿ Complete the sentences with the correct word or words.

1. You need to fill out an _____ to go through immigration.

2. Please listen to your boarding announcement in the _____ _____ area.

3. The flight attendant will give you a _____ to fill out.

4. A permanent _____ is someone who has been granted authorization to live and work in the United States on a permanent basis.

B : Useful Phrases

1. Are you   visiting Korea?
              a resident?

2. All passengers must fill out the customs form.
   Please fill out one customs form per family.
   You don't have to fill out any entry documents.

3. May I help you fill it(them) out?
   Would you like me to help you with it?

C : Conversation

1. Listen to the dialogues below and then practice them with your partner. (C: cabin crew / P: passenger)

Dialogue 1 (entry card – tourists entering Korea)

C : Excuse me. Are you visiting Korea?

P : Yes, I'll be staying for a week in Korea.

C : Then you have to fill out the arrival card and the customs form.

P : Okay. I'm traveling with my family. Should each of us complete the customs form?

C : No, sir. Just fill out one customs form per family, please.

P : I see, thanks.

C : You're welcome, sir.

Dialogue 2 (entry card – residents entering Korea)

C : Excuse me. Are you visiting Korea?

P : No, I'm not. I'm a resident.
When I left Korea, they put this embarkation card in my passport.
Do I need to fill it out again?

C : Then just fill in your flight number and the place of departure on the card.
And you need to fill out the customs form.

P : Okay, thanks.

Dialogue 3 (entry card –transit passengers)

C : Excuse me. These are the entry documents for Korea.

P : I'm just staying at the Incheon airport for a couple of hours.
Do I need to fill them out?

C : Then you don't have to fill out any entry documents.

Dialogue 4 (entry card – passengers entering USA)

C : Excuse me. Here's your customs form.

P : Is this the only form that I have to fill out?

C : Yes, ma'am. Foreign visitors no longer need to complete the arrival card.
May I help you fill it out?

P : That would be great.

2. Pair Work

Imagine that you and your partner are a member of the cabin crew and a passenger. Use the expressions provided above and continue the conversation by taking turns.

Cabin crew

Distribute an entry card to the passenger.

Help the passenger to fill out an entry card.

Passenger

Ask how to complete an entry card.

D : Build up

Match each question with the appropriate answer.

1. Are you visiting Korea?　•　　•　No, you don't have to.

2. Do I need to fill it out?　•　　•　That would be great.

3. May I help you fill it out?　•　　•　No, I'm a resident.

Unscramble the words to make sentences.

1. passengers   All   fill   arrival   out   card.   must   the

   ⇨ _____

2. have   You   to   fill   don't   out   documents.   any   entry

   ⇨ _____

3. your   Here's   form.   customs

   ⇨ _____

4. are   These   entry   Korea.   documents   the   for

   ⇨ _____

5. you   Would   you   like   to   it?   help   with   me

   ⇨ _____

E : Reading Comprehension

⚙ Read the text and answer the questions.

Arrival card

An arrival card is a legal document used by immigration authorities to provide passenger identification and a record of a person's entry into certain countries. It also provides information on health and character requirements for non-citizens entering a particular country.

Information on the card

The information requested varies by country. Typically the information requested on the departure card includes
- Full name
- Nationality
- Date of Birth
- Passport number, place of issuance and expiry date
- Flight number or name of aircraft, ship or vehicle
- Purpose of trip: vacation, education/study, visiting relatives/families, business, diplomatic
- Duration of stay
- Destination (next stop of disembarkation)
- Address in country
- Information on items being bought into the country which may be of interest to customs and quarantine authorities

Travelers are generally required to sign, date, and declare the information is true, correct, and complete.

Passengers on international flights are often required to complete the cards and are often required to present the cards and their passports at immigration checkpoints. Some countries, most notably those in the passport-free travel area of the Schengen Zone don't require travelers to complete this card.

Korea's Entry documents

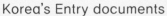

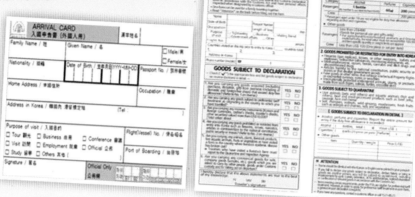

US Customs declaration card

en.wikipedia.org

1. What is an arrival card?

2. What information is required on the arrival card?

CHAPTER 03

Service before Landing

1. Preparation for landing

Service before Landing

착륙 전 업무

1) Approaching 방송 후

- 기내 방송 담당 승무원은 Approaching 방송을 실시한다.
- Headphone과 기내 잡지 등을 회수한다.
- 이륙 준비와 동일하게 객실 및 Galley의 안전 점검을 실시한다.

2) Landing 방송 후

- 기내 방송 담당 승무원은 Landing 방송을 실시한다.

- 승객의 착석, 좌석벨트 착용, 좌석 등받이와 Tray table, Arm rest, Foot rest의 정위치 등을 최종 확인 점검한다.
- 휴대 수하물 고정 및 Door side와 Aisle의 Clear 상태를 점검한다.
- 객실 및 Galley내 모든 Compartment와 Cart 등 유동물의 Locking 상태를 점검한다.
- 승무원은 안전 점검을 마친 후 지정된 Jump seat에 착석하여 좌석벨트와 Shoulder harness를 착용하고, 30 second review를 실시한다.

Preparation for landing

A : Words

✿ Match the words to the meanings.

flight	**on board**	**return**	**land**	**shortly**

1. _____ : on or in a ship, plane, or other vehicle

2. _____ : to bring an aircraft to the ground

3. _____ : a trip in an aircraft

4. _____ : in a short time

5. _____ : to go or come back to a previous place

✿ Complete the sentences with the correct word or words.

1. The flight landed _____ after 7 p.m.

2. The _____ flight of the aircraft was delayed due to bad weather.

3. The cabin crew were seeking a doctor _____ to help a woman who was in labor.

4. The airplane received clearance to _____ at Incheon International Airport.

B : Useful Phrases

1. Would you please

fasten(ing) your seatbelt?
return(ing) to your seat?
return(ing) your seatback to the upright position?
close(ing) your tray table?

   Would you mind (~ing)

put(ting) your bag in the overhead bins?
put(ting) your bag under the seat in front of you?
open(ing) your window shades?
hold(ing) your baby outside of your seatbelt?

2. May I take your

cup?
headphone?
bassinet down?

3. We'll be landing

shortly(soon).
in about _____ minutes.

4. ⎧the name⎫ is _____ hour(s)   behind   ⎧the name ⎫
   ⎩of the city⎭   ahead of ⎩of the city⎭.

C : Conversation

1. Listen to the dialogues below and then practice them with your partner. (C: cabin crew / P: passenger)

Dialogue 1 (Arrival information)

P : Excuse me, how long will it be before we get to Los Angeles?

C : We expect to arrive in about one hour.

P : What is the time difference between Seoul and Los Angeles?

C : Well, Los Angeles is 16 hours behind Seoul. We'll be arriving approximately 10 minutes ahead of schedule. So it would be 10 a.m. local time.

P : Alright, thank you.

C : My pleasure.

Dialogue 2 (Headphone collection)

C : Excuse me, sir. May I have your headphone, please? We'll be landing soon.

P : Oh! I'm still watching the movie.

C : If you are still using it, you may continue to do so.

P : Thank you.

C : You're welcome, sir.

Dialogue 3 (Used cup collection)

C : Excuse me. Are you finished with your drink?

P : Yes, I am.

C : May I take your cup?

P : Sure.

C : We'll be landing shortly.
Would you mind closing your tray table?

P : O.K.

Dialogue 4 (Safety check 1)

C : Excuse me, sir. We'll be landing soon. Would you please fasten your seatbelt and return your seatback to the upright position?

P : Okay.

C : And open your window shades, please.

P : I will.

C : Thank you, sir.

Dialogue 5 (Safety check 2)

C : Excuse me, ma'am. Did you have a nice flight?

P : Thanks to you, we had a wonderful flight.

C : Thank you very much. We'll be landing in about 15 minutes.
   May I take your bassinet down?

P : Sure, please.

C : … Would you please hold your baby outside of your seatbelt?
   It is much safer for your baby.

P : Oh, I see. Thank you.

C : You're welcome, ma'am.

Dialogue 6 (Baggage check 1)

C : Excuse me. Would you please put your bag in the overhead
   bins or under the seat in front of you? We'll be landing shortly.

P : Okay, I see.

C : Thank you.

Dialogue 7 (Baggage check 2)

C : Excuse me. Is this your bag, ma'am?

P : Yes, it is.

C : I'm sorry but we have to keep the aisle clear for the landing.
Would you mind keeping it under your seat?

P : Okay. I'll do that.

C : Thank you.

Dialogue 8 (Returning passenger's clothes)

P : Will you bring me my coat?

C : Certainly, sir. Just a moment, please. Here's your coat.

P : Thank you.

C : Did you enjoy your flight?

P : Yes, I did. I had a great time. Thank you.

C : You're welcome. I hope to see you on board again soon.

2. Pair Work

Imagine that you and your partner are a member of the cabin crew and a passenger. Use the expressions provided above and continue the conversation by taking turns.

Passenger

Ask about estimated time of arrival.

Ask about the time difference.

Cabin crew

Give detailed information about what the passenger asks.

D : Build up

✿ Fill in the blank with a right word from the box below.

clear	upright	in front of	continue

1. Would you please return your seatback to the _____ position?

2. If you are still using your headphone, you may _____ to do so.

3. Would you please put your bag under the seat _____ you?

4. I'm sorry but we have to keep the aisle _____ for the landing.

Match each question with the appropriate answer.

1. Are you finished with your drink?　　•　•Certainly, sir.

2. May I take your cup?　　•　•Yes, please.

3. Would you mind closing your tray table? •　•No, I don't.

4. Will you bring me my coat?　　•　•Yes, I am.

Unscramble the words to make sentences.

1. landing　We'll　shortly.　be

   ⇨ _____

2. shades?　open　Would　please　window　you　your

   ⇨ _____

3. minutes.　We'll　about　landing　20　be　in

   ⇨ _____

4. hold your baby　your seatbelt?　outside of　Would you please

   ⇨ _____

E : Reading Comprehension

✿ Read the text and answer the questions.

Preparation for landing – In-flight passenger announcements

© www.hanol.co.kr

Before, or during the descent, the Captain will usually make an announcement with local time and temperature at the destination airport, and time left until arrival. It is followed by an announcement from the flight attendant.

"Ladies and gentlemen, as we start our descent, please make sure your seat backs and tray tables are in their full upright position. Make sure your seat belt is securely fastened and all carry-on luggage is stowed underneath the seat in front of you or in the overhead bins. Thank you."

To indicate the landing clearance or final approach, the Captain will either make the following announcement and/or blink the No Smoking sign.

> "Flight attendants, prepare for landing please."
> "Cabin crew, please take your seats for landing."

It may be followed by an announcement by a flight attendant.

> "Ladies and gentlemen, we have just been cleared to land at Los Angeles International airport. Please make sure one last time your seat belt is securely fastened. The flight attendants are currently passing around the cabin to make a final compliance check and pick up any remaining cups and glasses. Thank you."

www.airodyssey.net

1. Before the descent, what information does the captain deliver in his announcement?

2. What should passengers do for their safety before landing?

CHAPTER 04

After Landing

1. Arrival

After Landing

1. Taxing 중 업무

1) Farewell 방송 실시

기내방송 담당 승무원은 착륙 후 엔진의 역회전(Engine reverse)가 끝난 시점에 Farewell(환송) 방송을 실시한다.

2) 승객 착석 유지

- 승무원은 승객의 안전을 위해 Taxing 중 Fasten seatbelt sign이 꺼질 때까지 반드시 승객의 착석을 유지하도록 해야 한다.
- 필요 시 객실 사무장은 Gate 진입 직전 Taxing 중 승객 착석 요청 방송을 실시한다.

2. Safety check 및 승객 하기 협조

1) Safety check 후 Door open

- 사무장의 Safety check 방송에 따라 전 승무원은 담당 Door의 Slide mode를 정상 위치로 변경하고 상호 확인 후 사무장에게 보고한다.
- 사무장은 Door open 후 운송담당 직원에게 Ship pouch를 인계하고, 특별 승객, 운송 제한 승객 등 업무 수행에 관한 필요사항을 전달한다.

2) 승객 하기

- 승무원은 승객 하기 시 각자의 담당 구역별로 Jump seat 주변에서 승객에게 하기 인사를 하고, 승객 하기가 원활하게 진행되도록 협조한다.
- UM, 장애인 승객, 유아 동반 승객, 노약자 승객, 운송 제한 승객 등 도움이 필요한 승객의 하기에 협조한다.

1 Arrival

A : Words

Match the words to the meanings.

arrive   parking area   enjoy   deplane

1. _____ : an outside area where vehicles are parked

2. _____ : come to a destination at the end of a journey

3. _____ : to leave an airplane

4. _____ : to get pleasure from something

Complete the sentences with the correct word or words.

1. Please sit back, relax, and _____ the flight.

2. The _____s at the Terminal 2 are not available at the moment.

3. Please make sure to take all your personal belongings with you as you _____.

4. Please stay in your seat until we _____ at the gate.

B : Useful Phrases

1. Would you please remain seated until the plane

   completely stops?

   comes to a complete stop?

2. Did you enjoy the flight?

   have a pleasant flight today?

3. I hope you have a wonderful time in Korea.

   enjoy your stay in Seoul.

   have a pleasant stay in Korea.

4. I hope to see you again soon.

   to see you on board again.

   you fly with us again in the future.

C : Conversation

1. Listen to the dialogues below and then practice them with your partner. (C: cabin crew / P: passenger)

Dialogue 1 (During taxing after landing)

C : Excuse me, sir. We've not reached the parking area yet. Would you please remain seated until the plane completely stops?

P : Oh, I thought we had arrived at the gate. Why aren't we moving?

C : We're waiting for another plane to depart.

P : Okay.

© www.hanol.co.kr

Dialogue 2 (Returning passengers' baggage)

C : Excuse me, ma'am. Here's your bag.

P : Oh, thank you.

C : You're welcome, ma'am. Did you enjoy the flight?

P : Yes, it was great.

C : I'm very glad to hear that. I hope you have a wonderful time in Korea.

Dialogue 3 (Assisting passengers' baggage)

C : May I help you with your bags, ma'am?

P : No, thank you. I can manage.

C : Alright. I hope you enjoy your stay in Seoul. Good bye, ma'am.

Dialogue 4 (Upper deck passengers' deplaning)

C : I'm sorry but would you mind waiting here while the passengers in the upper deck are coming down?

P1 : Okay, I see.

C : Thank you for your cooperation.
(to P2) Watch your step, please. Goodbye. …
(to P1) I'm sorry to have kept you waiting. Now you may deplane. This way, please.

P1 : Alright, thanks.

C : Thank you for flying with us. Goodbye.

Dialogue 5 (Saying goodbye)

C : How was your flight?

P : It was wonderful. I had a very good time with you. Thank you.

C : I'm so glad to hear that. I hope to see you on board again.
　　Have a pleasant stay in Korea.

2.　Pair Work

Imagine that you and your partner are a member of the cabin crew and a passenger. Use the expressions provided above and continue the conversation by taking turns.

Passenger

1. Ask why the airplane stops.

2. Say goodbye to the cabin crew.

Cabin crew

1. Explain why the airplane isn't moving.

2. Ask the passenger if he/she enjoys the flight or not.

3. Say goodbye to the passenger.

D : Build up

❁ Fill in the blank with a right word from the box below.

| stay | completely | parking area | depart |

1. Would you please remain seated until the plane _____ stops?

2. We're waiting for another plane to _____.

3. I hope you enjoy your _____ in Seoul.

4. We've not reached the _____ yet.

❁ Unscramble the words to make sentences.

1. flight? Did enjoy you the

   ⇨ _____

2. I you help May with bags? your

   ⇨ _____

3. you Thank us. for with flying

   ⇨ _____

4. board I to hope again. see you on

   ⇨ _____

5. pleasant Have Korea. stay in a

   ⇨ _____

E : Reading Comprehension

Read the text and answer the questions.

Automated Immigration at Incheon Airport

Departure/Arrivals immigration processing is simpler and quicker.

Eligible Passengers and Period

- Eligible Passengers: Holders of Korean Resident Registration Cards over the age of 17 (Passengers over the age of 14 but under 17 must receive parental consent and submit identity documents)
- Eligibility Period: Valid until one 1 day before the expiration date
- Registered Aliens: Must meet certain conditions (permanent residence, investor, etc.)

Automated Immigration Processing Registration Center (032–740–7400~1)

- In front of Check-in Counter F on Passenger Terminal 3rd Floor
- Hours of Operation: 07:00-19:00 (Open all-year)
- You can register at the manned immigration checkpoints as well. (08:00-19:00).

Enroll procedure of Automated Immigration

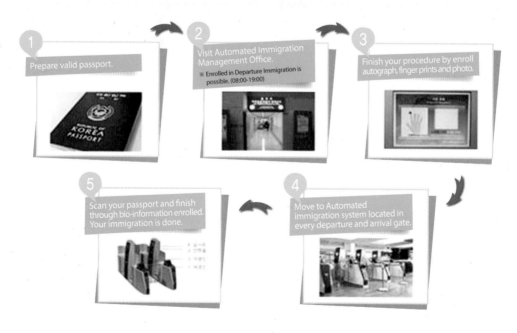

Pass through Automated Immigration machine

1 Scan your passport.

2 Pass through opened door.

3 Identify yourself by fingerprints.

5 Pass through opened door. Your immigration is finished.

4 Identify yourself by face photo.

www.airport.kr

1. What do you enroll when you complete the Automated Immigration procedure?

2. Decide whether the statements are true or false.

   1) Holders of Korean resident registration cards over the age of 17 are eligible. (   )

   2) It is valid until the day of the expiration date. (   )

   3) Automated immigration processing registration center opens all-year round. (   )

05

Handling Sick Passengers

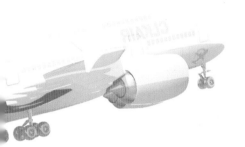

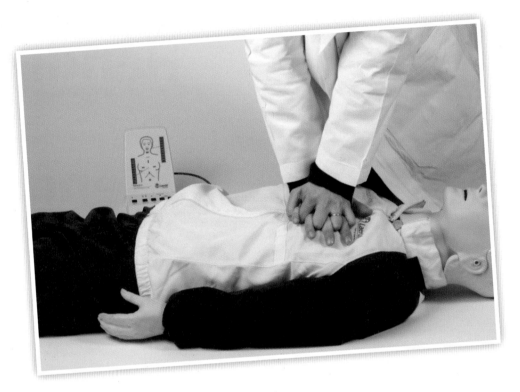

응급환자 발생 시 대처 요령

1) 상황 판단

최소 2명 이상의 승무원이 신속하게 상황을 판단 후 조치를 취함

승객안정 ➡ 도움 필요 여부 확인 ➡ 상황 파악 및 환자에 대한 의학 정보 습득 ➡ 의사소견서 확인

2) Communication

도움 요청 및 응급처치 장비 준비 ➡ 기장에게 통보 ➡ 사무장에 의한 Doctor paging 방송 실시 ➡ 필요시 지상 의료진과의 의사소통

3) ABC Servey

기도(Airway)유지 확인 ➡ 호흡(Breathing) 확인 ➡ 심장 박동(Circulation) 확인

4) Secondary Servey

- 발병 당시 환자의 상태가 위중하지는 않지만 위급한 상황으로 진행될 수 있는 질병을 미연에 방지하는 절차
- 응급환자와 주변 승객들 면담, 활력징후(맥박, 호흡, 혈압, 체온)와 피부색 변화 관찰, 환자의 상처, 질병, 건강상태를 계속 확인, 응급처치 내용을 순서대로 기록

5) EMCS(Emergency Medical Call System)

비행 중인 항공기에서 응급환자 발생시 지상에 대기하고 있는 의료진과 연락하여 연계진료가 가능하도록 만든 제도

6) 기내 응급처치 장비

- EMK(Emergency Medical Kit) : 응급환자 발생시 의료진에 의한 전문적인 치료를 위해 탑재되어 의료인(의사, 한의사, 치과의사, 간호사, 조산사)만 사용 가능
- FAK(First Aid Kit) : 일반적인 구급 상자로 50석당 1개가 봉인된 채로 탑재
- Medical Bag : 객실 승무원이 소지하고 있는 상비약
- AED(Automated External Defibrillator) : 호흡과 맥박이 없는 심장 질환 환자에게 전기충격을 주어 심장 기능을 복구할 수 있도록 도와주는 의료기구
- Resuscitator Bag : 인공 호흡이 어려울 때 사용하는 기구
- UPK(Universal Precaution Kit) : 환자의 체액이나 타액으로부터 오염을 방지해주는 장비
- PO2 bottle : 휴대용 산소통
- 자동 혈압계, 혈당 측정기, 청진기, 혈압계, 얼음찜질 팩 등

1 Handling Sick Passengers

A : Words

Match the words to the meanings.

| sore throat | airsickness | allergy | medicine | indigestion |

1. _____ : having a feeling of nausea due to travel in an aircraft

2. _____ : treatment for disease or illness

3. _____ : an abnormal reaction of a body to a certain foods, pollen, fur, or dust

4. _____ : pain and discomfort in the stomach caused by difficulties in digesting food

5. _____ : a pain, itchiness, or irritation of the throat

Complete the sentences with the correct word or words.

1. Peanuts are one of the most common _____-causing foods.

2. You need to check what rules apply to taking your _____ out of the country or into the country you're going to.

3. I had a really bad _____ after a long flight.

4. _____ symptoms include nausea, vomiting, dizziness, and sweating.

5. Air travel can make you more likely to suffer from _____.

B : Useful Phrases

1. Do you have any allergies to the medicine?
   Are you allergic to any medicine?

2. I'll | get it for you | right away.
       | I'll bring it to you | immediately.

3. I hope you | feel better | soon.
              | get well |

4. If there is anything I can do for you, just let me know.
   If you need anything else, let me know.
   Is there anything I can do for you?

5. I'm | sorry | to hear that.
       | glad |

C : Conversation

1. Listen to the dialogues below and then practice them with your partner. (C: cabin crew / P: passenger)

Dialogue 1 (Airsickness)

C : Excuse, me, ma'am. Are you alright?

P : No, I don't think so. I feel like I'm going to throw up.

C : Please use this airsickness bag if you need, ma'am.
    Is there anything I can do for you?

P : Do you have any medicine for airsickness?

C : Yes, we do. Are you allergic to any medicine?

P : No, I'm not.

C : Just a moment, please. I'll get it for you.
    … Here is your medicine.
    I hope you feel better soon.

Dialogue 2 (Headache)

P : Excuse, me. Do you have any medicine for headaches?
I have a terrible headache.

C : Oh, that's too bad. We have Tylenol.
Do you have any allergies to the medicine?

P : No, I don't.

C : Alright. I'll bring it to you immediately.
… Here's your Tylenol and a glass of water.
Please take two pills.

P : Okay, thanks.

C : You're welcome. I hope you get well soon.
(After a while) How are you feeling now?

P : I feel much better now. Thank you.

C : I'm so glad to hear that. If there is anything I can do for you,
just let me know.

© www.hanol.co.kr

Dialogue 3 (Indigestion)

C : Excuse me, sir. Are you alright? You look uncomfortable.

P : I have really bad indigestion.
Do you have anything I can take?

C : Yes, we do. We have medicine called Beaje on board.
Are you allergic to any medicine?

P : No, I'm not. Can I have some?

C : Certainly, sir. Just a moment, please.
… Here you are. I hope you get well soon.

Dialogue 4 (Sore throat)

P : Excuse me. It is so dry in here and I have a sore throat.
Do you have anything for that?

C : Oh, I'm sorry to hear that. But I'm afraid we don't have that
medicine but we have some medicine for a common cold.
Would you like to try that?

P : That would be good.

C : Just a moment, please. I'll get it for you right away.

2. Pair Work

Imagine that you and your partner are a member of the cabin crew and a passenger. Use the expressions provided above and continue the conversation by taking turns.

Passenger

1. Tell the cabin crew you feel sick.

2. Tell the cabin crew you have a sore throat.

Cabin crew

1. Bring the passenger proper medicine.

2. Tell the passenger the medicine that he/she asks for is not available and provide alternative medicine.

D : Build up

Fill in the blank with a right word from the box below.

| allergic | airsickness bag | medicine | immediately |

1. Please use this _____ if you need.

2. Are you _____ to any medicine?

3. I'll bring it to you _____.

4. I'm afraid we don't have any _____ for a sore throat.

Unscramble the words to make sentences.

1. feel   I   soon.   you   hope   better

   ⇨ _____

2. any   Do   headache?   you   medicine   have   for

   ⇨ _____

3. now?   are   How   feeling   you

   ⇨ _____

4. there   If   is   know.   anything   I   let   do   for   can   you,   just   me

   ⇨ _____

5. hear   I'm   that.   to   sorry

   ⇨ _____

E : Reading Comprehension

Read the text and answer the questions.

Medical emergencies in the sky
What happens if you get ill on a plane?

written by A. Pawlowski

© www.hanol.co.kr

Medical emergencies in the sky happen every day. What kind of treatment can you expect if you pass out, choke or otherwise become unwell at 35,000 feet?

About 44,000 in-flight medical emergencies take place worldwide each year, according to a 2013 study in The New England Journal of Medicine.

Some of its findings are sobering: If you were to suffer a heart attack, seizure or other health problem on a plane, "access to care is limited," the authors write. Thankfully, serious illness is rare. The most common in-flight health issues include fainting, respiratory problems and nausea or vomiting. If you get sick, your first responders will be members of the crew. Flight attendants are trained to handle medical emergencies and planes are equipped with first aid kits. They can also administer CPR.

Is there a doctor on board?

The FAA requires defibrillators and emergency medical kits on planes that can carry more than 30 passengers. The kits include medicines such as nitroglycerin tablets, which can relieve chest pain, and dextrose, to treat low blood sugar.

Only a licensed medical professional can use many of the items inside the kit, which is why you will hear flight attendants page for a doctor.

Doctors may be reluctant for many reasons. Providing care in a cramped, noisy cabin can be daunting. With little equipment and no knowledge of the patient's medical history, some physicians may also be worried about getting sued.

Sometimes, the emergency requires returning to the ground.

On domestic routes, the pilot can usually land in 15 minutes if it's necessary to divert the flight because someone is seriously ill. It's a different story on international routes, when a plane might be over an ocean and hours away from an airport.

But it turns out most health problems can be successfully treated on board: only 7 percent of flights with medical emergencies had to divert in The New England Journal of Medicine study.

The emergencies can be hard on flight attendants, too.

Heather Poole, a veteran flight attendant for a major U.S. airline remembers rushing to a passenger who passed out and then suddenly regained consciousness during meal service on an international flight.

"It's not easy to smile and serve passengers, and then out of nowhere have to deal with an almost dead passenger, and then go right back to smiling and serving passengers. My heart was pounding like crazy after that," Poole recalled.

www.today.com

1. Decide whether the statements are true or false.

   1) The most common in-flight health issues include a heart attack and seizure. (   )

   2) Only a licensed medical professional can use many of the items inside the emergency medical kits on planes. (   )

   3) Flight attendants are trained to administer CPR. (   )

   4) Doctors are willing to provide emergency medical care for the patients on board. (   )

   5) Most health problems can be successfully treated in the cabin. (   )

Answer Keys

Chapter 1. Boarding & Service before Takeoff

1. Boarding

A. Words

1. passenger 2. cabin 3. aisle 4. boarding 5. welcome 6. upstairs 7. aircraft

1. passenger 2. aisle 3. boarding 4. aircraft 5. welcomed

D. Build up

*1. boarding pass 2. flight 3. aisle 4. cabin 5. front

*1. It's 16A. 2. Yes, here you are. 3. Please take the other aisle..

*1. May I see your boarding pass, please?

2. Please take the other aisle on your left.

3. Your seat is in the front of the cabin on your left.

4. Please use those stairs and watch your step.

5. Would you please step aside to let these people through?

6. We have to recheck your boarding pass individually for security.

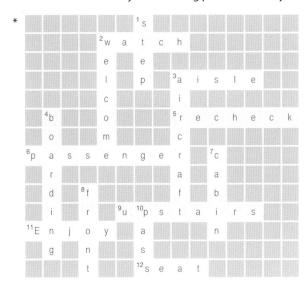

E. Reading Comprehension

1. It is the action of getting onto an airplane.

2. It can start any time from thirty minutes to twenty minutes before scheduled departure.

3. checking validity of passenger boarding passes, assisting passengers with seat assignments, monitoring cabin baggage and electronic devices, ensuring exit seat criterias are met, monitoring child restraint devices as well as keeping a visual watch of the cabin at all times

2. Baggage securing

A. Words

1. overhead bin 2. seat 3. coatroom 4. compartment 5. baggage

1. seat 2. coatroom 3. compartment 4.baggage

D. Build up

*1.help 2. overhead 3. putting 4. understanding 5. store

*1. We have to keep the aisle clear during the flight.

  2. If you need anything during the flight, please let me know.

  3. I'll keep it in the coatroom in the front of the cabin.

  4. Would you please put them in the overhead bin?

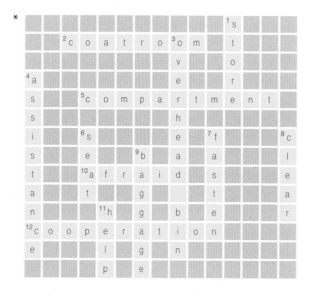

E. Reading Comprehension

1. Each traveler can bring on board one carry-on bag plus one personal item on free of charge.

2. The maximum size (width + heights + depth) is 158cm/62in and the maximum weight per bag is 23kg/ 50lb or 32kg/70lb depending on your ticket class and itineraries.

3. All carry-ons must be able to be stored completely in an overhead bin or under the seat in front of you.

3. Seating arrangement

A. Words

1. separate 2. assignment 3. arrange 4. occupy 5. inconvenience 6. empty

1. separate 2. inconvenience 3. arrange 4. occupy 5. assignment

D. Build up

*1. separate 2. behind 3. rearranged 4. inconvenience

*1. We have some seats available in the back of the cabin.

  2. I'm afraid there has been a mistake in the seating arrangement.

3. Would you mind waiting here for a moment while I check on this?

4. If you need anything during the flight, please let me know.

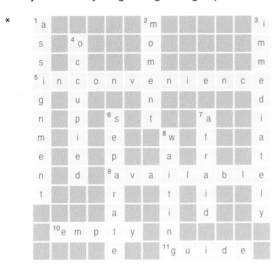

E. Reading Comprehension

1. If you sit on an aisle seat, you can stretch your legs during the flight but you can be disturbed if the person in the window seat wants to get out. If you sit on a window seat, you can be undisturbed.

2. Passengers sitting near the exit doors must assist cabin crew in case of emergencies.

4. Ground service

A. Words

1. valuables 2. available 3. return 4. armrest 5. coatroom 6. bassinet

1. return 2. bassinet 3. coatroom 4. valuables 5. available

D. Build up

*1. request 2. set up 3. return 4. valuables 5. inconvenience 6. instead

*1. Certainly. Do you have any valuables in your coat?

2. Yes, I did.

3. Sure, here it is.

4. Yes, sir. I'll bring them for you right away.

*1. Would you like to have a baby bassinet for your baby?

2. If you need anything, just let me know.

3. Is there anything I can do for you ma'am?

4. I'll get you another one right away.

5. The Washington Post is not available on this flight.

6. Would you like to read a newspaper?

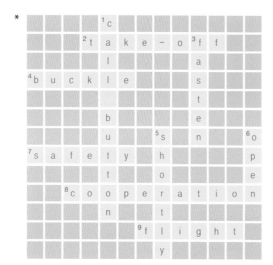

E. Reading Comprehension

1. It should be ordered until 24 hours (Kosher meals: until 48 hours) before departure.

2. 1) F   2) T   3) F   4) T

5. Preparing for take-off

A. Words

1. fasten   2. seatback   3. upright   4. take off   5. safety   6. electronic devices   7. seatbelt

1. seatback   2. Safety   3. take off   4. electronic devices   5. upright   6. Fasten

D. Build up

*1. seatbelt   2. closing   3. taking off   4. call button   5. comfortable

*1. Please return your seatback to the upright position.

2. Would you please hold your baby outside of your seatbelt?

3. Will you show me how to fasten my seatbelt?

4. You can use it again after take-off.

E. Reading Comprehension

1. We must return to our seat and fasten our seat belt securely.

2. Fasten your seat belt. Put away your tray table. Return your seat back to the upright position.

Chapter 2. In-flight Service

1. Beverage and Meal service

A. Words

1. recommend   2. on the rocks   3. selection   4. apology   5. kosher meal   6. liqueur   7. entrée

1. entrée   2. on the rocks   3. recommend   4. apology   5. selection

D. Build up

*1. kosher meal   2. understanding   3. apology   4. afraid   5. wipe

*1. Yes, I did.   2. Yes, please.   3. I'll have beef.   4. Not yet.   5. On the rocks, please.

*1. We're serving lunch now.

2. Would you please open your tray table?

3. Would you care for another drink?

4. I'm sorry but I'm afraid I don't know how it's made.

5. It's made of vodka and orange juice.

*
```
  ¹c ²a  r  ³e
     d     n                        ⁴s
     d     t           ⁵m  a  d  e
     r                             r
     e           ⁶r              v
⁷c a r  e ⁸f  u  l        e        i
          i              c        n
       ⁹l  n    ¹⁰a p  o  l  o  g  y
     ¹¹m i  x  i  n  g    m
       q     s           m
       u     h     ¹²w  e
     ¹³s e  l  e  c  t  i  o  n
       u     d     p     d
       r           e
```

E. Reading Comprehension

1. We receive a nice hot towel for refreshment and an aperitif with nuts.

2. We can get snacks, ice cream or a sandwich.

3. 1) T   2) F   3) F

2. In-flight sales

A. Words

   1. duty free 2. liquor 3. purchase 4. accept 5. change 6. receipt 7. allowance

   1. duty free 2. receipt 3. purchase 4. liquor

D. Build up

   *1. information 2. allowed 3. run out of 4. change 5. accept

   *1. I need some whisky.

    2. I'll pay by credit card.

    3. It is not available since we are preparing for landing.

    4. Certainly, ma'am.

   *1. Would you like something else, instead?

    2. Could I have your signature, please?

    3. The total comes to 100 US dollars.

    4. I'm very sorry to have kept you waiting.

    5. I'm afraid it is not available since we are preparing for landing.

    6. Thank you for your understanding.

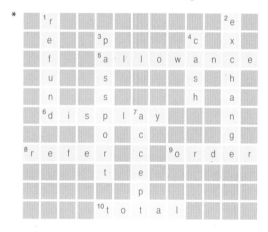

E. Reading Comprehension

   1. Shopping Extravaganza

   2. 1) F 2) T

3. Handling complaints and requests

A. Words

   1. temperature 2. pressure 3. cooperation 4. assistance 5. lavatory 6. aviation law

   1. aviation law 2. lavatory 3. pressure 4. assistance

D. Build up

   *1. temperature 2. smoking 3. assistance 4. instead 5. mistake

   *1. I'm so sorry for the inconvenience.

    2. I'll heat it up for you immediately.

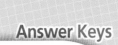

3. Would you like some bread while you are waiting?

4. I'll get you another meal right away.

5. I'll check on your meal immediately.

*

				¹l		²d	³i	s	t	¹⁰a	n	c	e
				i			n			v			
			⁴r		q		c			o			
			e		u		o			d			
			⁵s	m	o	k	i	n	g				
		⁶a		e		r		v					
		p		t		⁷m	e	a	l				
		o					n						
		l		⁸a	s	s	i	s	t	a	n	c	e
		o				e							
⁹v	e	g	e	t	a	r	i	a	n				
		y				c							
						e							

E. Reading Comprehension

1. Take a step back. Give the customer your full attention and listen to the whole problem before responding. Give a sincere apology immediately. Try to find a solution.

2. 1) T   2) F   3) T

4. Entry documents

A. Words

1. arrival card 2.customs form 3.complete 4.resident 5.embarkation 6.transit 7.visitors

1. arrival card 2. transit 3. customs form 4. resident

D. Build up

*1. No, I'm a resident. 2. No, you don't have to. 3. That would be great.

*1. All passengers must fill out the arrival card.

2. You don't have to fill out any entry documents.

3. Here's your customs form.

4. These are the entry documents for Korea.

5. Would you like me to help you with it?

E. Reading Comprehension

1. It is a legal document used by immigration authorities to provide passenger identification and a record of a person's entry into certain countries.

2. Full name, Nationality, Date of Birth, Passport number, place of issuance and expiry date, Flight number or name of aircraft, ship or vehicle, Purpose of trip, Duration of stay, Destination (next stop of disembarkation), Address in country, Information on items being bought into the country which may be of interest to customs and quarantine authorities.

Chapter 3. Service before Landing

1. Preparation for landing

A. Words

  1. on board 2. land 3. flight 4. shortly 5. return

  1. shortly 2. return 3. on board 4. land

D. Build up

  *1. upright 2. continue 3. in front of 4. clear

  *1. Yes, I am. 2. Yes, please. 3. No, I don't. 4. Certainly, sir.

  *1. We'll be landing shortly.

   2. Would you please open your window shades?

   3. We'll be landing in about 15 minutes.

   4. Would you please hold your baby outside of your seatbelt?

E. Reading Comprehension

  1. The Captain will usually make an announcement with local time and temperature at the destination airport, and time left until arrival.

  2. Passengers must fasten their seatbelts, return their seatback to the upright position, and make sure all carry-on luggage is stowed underneath the seat in front of them or in the overhead bins.

Chapter 4. After Landing

1. Arrival

A. Words

  1. parking area 2. arrive 3. deplane 4. enjoy

  1. enjoy 2. parking area 3. deplane 4. arrive

D. Build up

  *1. completely 2. depart 3. stay 4. parking area

  *1. Did you enjoy the flight?

   2. May I help you with your bags?

   3. Thank you for flying with us.

   4. I hope to see you on board again.

   5. Have a pleasant stay in Korea.

E. Reading Comprehension

  1. Enroll autograph, finger prints and photo.

  2. 1) T 2) F 3) T

Chapter 5. Handling Sick Passengers

1. Handling Sick Passengers

A. Words

   1. airsickness 2. medicine 3. allergy 4. indigestion 5. a sore throat

   1. allergy 2. medicine 3. sore throat 4. airsickness 5. indigestion

D. Build up

   *1. airsickness bag 2. allergic 3. immediately 4. medicine

   * 1. I hope you feel better soon.

    2. Do you have any medicine for headache?

    3. How are you feeling now?

    4. If there is anything I can do for you, just let me know.

    5. I'm sorry to hear that.

E. Reading Comprehension

   1. 1) F 2) T 3) T 4) F 5) T

Essential English for Cabin Crew, 왕수명, 박윤미, Richard Whitten 저, 동양북스

NCS기반 항공객실서비스 영어, 이효선 저, 지식인

Practical English for flight attendants, 김현수, Reashelle Braiden 저, 백산출판사

Real English for Cabin Crew (실무편), Jina Myong, Eun Lee 저, 다락원

대한항공 신입전문훈련 영어교재

응급환자 대처, 최성수 저, 한올출판사

항공객실업무, 박혜정 저, 백산출판사

저자 소개

마근정

- 고려대학교 영어영문학과 졸업
- 명지대학교 교육대학원 교육학석사 (영어교육 전공)

- 연성대학교 강의전담전임교수(2021~현재)
- 연성대학교 항공서비스과 겸임교수 (2012~2020)
  - 연성대학교 우수강의 교수상 수상 (2016, 2020)
- 부천대학교 비서사무행정과 겸임교수 (2019)
- 재능대학교 항공운항서비스과 외래교수 (2013)

- 저서
  - 영문법과 영작문 한방에 끝내기 1(2020)
  - 영문법과 영작문 한방에 끝내기 2(2020)
  - 승무원 영어면접 한방에 끝내기 초판(2016), 2판(2019)
  - Practical English for Airline Service(2017)
  - NCS기반 항공 기내방송 업무(2016)

- ㈜대한항공 객실 사무장 (1999~2010)
  - 객실훈련원 Regional flight attendants(동남아 현지 승무원) 서비스 강사
  - 객실훈련원 기내방송 강사(기내방송 한국어, 영어, 일어 A자격 보유)
  - 객실훈련원 중국 남방항공 사무장 서비스 위탁 교육 진행
  - 객실승무원 신입 및 경력직 입사 면접위원
  - Mercury Award(ITCA) : Flying Mom 서비스 프레젠테이션 실시, 금상 수상(2007)
  - Avion Award(WAEA) : 기내엔터테인먼트 관련 프레젠테이션 실시, 최고성과상 수상(2007)
  - 사장표창 3회 (FR/CL 교육성적 우수, 특별사업수행모범)
  - VIP 전용기 Gulfstream 담당 승무원
  - SkyTeam Ambassador
  - SkyTeam Product Fair in Italy 행사 진행
  - '비' 월드투어 시드니 콘서트 행사 진행
  - 2002 월드컵 홍보관

Practical English for Airline Service

초판1쇄 발행 2017년 8월 25일
수정1쇄 발행 2021년 8월 20일

지은이   마 근 정
펴낸이   임 순 재

펴낸곳   (주)한올출판사
등 록   제11-403호
주 소   서울시 마포구 모래내로 83(성산동, 한올빌딩 3층)
전 화   (02)376-4298(대표)
팩 스   (02)302-8073
홈페이지   www.hanol.co.kr
e-메일   hanol@hanol.co.kr

ISBN 979-11-6647-113-1